Pastoral Care from a Third World Perspective

Research in Religion and Family
Black Perspectives

Noel Leo Erskine
General Editor

Vol. 6

PETER LANG
New York • Washington, D.C./Baltimore • Bern
Frankfurt am Main • Berlin • Brussels • Vienna • Oxford

Tapiwa N. Mucherera

Pastoral Care from a Third World Perspective

A Pastoral Theology of Care for the Urban Contemporary Shona in Zimbabwe

PETER LANG
New York • Washington, D.C./Baltimore • Bern
Frankfurt am Main • Berlin • Brussels • Vienna • Oxford

Library of Congress Cataloging-in-Publication Data

Mucherera, Tapiwa N.
Pastoral care from a Third World perspective: a pastoral theology of
care for the urban contemporary Shona in Zimbabwe / Tapiwa N. Mucherera.
p. cm. — (Research in religion and family; vol. 6)
Includes bibliographical references (p.) and index.
1. Pastoral counseling—Zimbabwe. 2. Shona—
Pastoral counseling. I. Title. II. Series.
BV4012.2 .M83 253'.096894—dc21 2001029275
ISBN 0-8204-5250-5
ISSN 1055-1158

Die Deutsche Bibliothek-CIP-Einheitsaufnahme

Mucherera, Tapiwa N.:
Pastoral care from a Third World perspective: a pastoral theology of
care for the urban contemporary shona in Zimbabwe / Tapiwa N. Mucherera.
–New York; Washington, D.C./Baltimore; Bern;
Frankfurt am Main; Berlin; Brussels; Vienna; Oxford: Lang.
(Research in religion and family; Vol. 6)
ISBN 0-8204-5250-5

The paper in this book meets the guidelines for permanence and durability
of the Committee on Production Guidelines for Book Longevity
of the Council of Library Resources.

Printed in the United States of America

TABLE OF CONTENTS

ACKNOWLEDGMENTS

I thank Asbury Theological Seminary for providing me with the necessary financial support needed for the publication of this book. Dr. Joel Green, thanks for all your encouragement in the process.

This book was originally published as my dissertation project. Special appreciation to those who worked with me on the original project, Drs. Joretta Marshall, Sandra Dixon and Edward Antonio.

In my academic journey, I have been taught by many teachers who influenced my thinking in terms of Pastoral Theology of Care. Many thanks to Drs. P.U.M.Mlambo, Edward Wimberly, Larry Graham and Archie Smith to name a few. Outside of the field of Pastoral Care: Drs. Gwinyai H. Muzorewa, George Tinker, Teresia Hinga and Art Jones, thank you.

I thank my parents Tracy and Gandidzwana, for believing in me and being able to acknowledge the gifts and graces God gave me. This book is partly a product of those things you taught me. My late auntie Naomi Mundondo, and grandmother Chemunoisa, were some of my greatest teachers. Mrs. Zvinoira (John), and other teachers I cannot all list, thanks.

Above all, thanks to my wife Bertha, sister in-law Zviko, niece Faro, and my children, Shamiso, Anesu and Ruvimbo for every little bit of support and hugs gave me through out. Dr. Eliakim Sibanda, my friend, thanks for your necessary criticism and feedback you gave. You are a star.

Annie Reed and Carol Swego thanks for your tirelessness in helping me with the final editing of this work. My series editor Dr. Noel Leo Erskine thanks for your great feedback and recommendations. Thanks to everyone else I might have overlooked. Ultimately, glory, honor and thanks be to God, through Christ!

CHAPTER ONE

Introduction: Continuity and Change in an African Context

Ziva kwawakabva is a Shona saying which translates as, "Know your history, your roots, or from where you came." Chidyausiku, a Shona writer, says, "Only a foolish generation forgets its history. Those who forget their history are doomed to repeat it. Worse still is that generation which not only forgets but mutilates its heritage."[1] The Shonas believe that one's history influences who one is and who one becomes, making the above statement important for them. Shonas believe that one's blood relations (extended family relations), as well as communal interpersonal relations and place of origin, have a great impact on one's life.

Due to arbitrary boundaries imposed by the British in the 1800s, the Shona people are mainly found in Zimbabwe, and in some of its neighboring countries; the Shona are part of the Bantu African group. Bantus are known as such because of their similar history of origin and some common meanings of words in the Bantu languages. Zimbabwe is located on the southern central part of the African continent. Its independence was gained from White (British) minority rule in 1980. Zimbabwe, colonized by the British in 1890, was formerly named after Cecil John Rhodes, and was known as Rhodesia.

This book addresses issues within pastoral theology of care in the African context, specifically in the urban Shona context. The following

1 Paul Chidyausiku, *Broken Roots: A Biographical Narrative on the Culture of the Shona People in Zimbabwe* (Gweru: Mambo Press, 1984), vii.

case study (cited later with greater detail) illustrates the issues of individuals caught between two opposing cultures and religions. More specifically, the case study highlights the personal and religious identity issues faced in the urban contemporary Shona context.[2] The case study illustrates the thesis of this book: in order for pastoral theology of care to be relevant in the contemporary urban Shona Christian context, pastors serving in this context must be equipped with a pastoral theological and psychodynamic understanding of integrative consciousness.

Nhamo and Netsai are a young couple in their thirties. They live in one of the suburbs of Harare. Nhamo is an independent person who owns a very successful business and who has assimilated many Western cultural and economic values. The couple decided to consult their pastor after experiencing the continual illness of their son, difficulties in their marriage, and the husband's depression. Netsai grew up in a family that held African traditional religious and cultural values. Nhamo's family of origin was comfortable mixing African traditional religion and Christianity. Nhamo attended a mission school where he was not exposed to much African traditional religion; he converted to Christianity when he was attending the university.

According to Nhamo and Netsai, their problem started when Nhamo went to introduce Netsai to his parents. Nhamo's father openly rejected Nhamo's intentions to marry Netsai. Nhamo's father said he had heard that Netsai's family was accused of being witches and that the family was being hounded by a *ngozi* spirit. Nhamo asked his father to reconsider. The father agreed and called the extended family for a meeting to address Nhamo's request.

At the meeting, Nhamo's father restated his reasons for rejecting Nhamo's proposed marriage. Nhamo became angry and started speaking in English. The uncles and grandfather registered their complaint, saying that they felt disrespected by Nhamo and could not help him since he was speaking in English. He ignored them and told them they (including the father) were neither good Christians nor sufficiently educated. The father told Nhamo he held a grudge against him for the things Nhamo had said. In

2 The illustrative case reflects the type of situations which urban pastoral caregivers must address. Analysis will be presented in the fifth chapter.

addition, the father suggested Nhamo look for a new father. Nhamo ignored all advice he was given by his family and married Netsai.

When the couple moved into their suburban home, they found a horn filled with blood in a tree next to their bedroom window.[3] They invited some church members for a prayer meeting and burned the horn. The horn, however, did not burn. Nhamo and Netsai did not perceive this to have any significant meaning.

The couple's first pregnancy ended in a miscarriage, despite the fact that Netsai received prenatal care. Zvitendo (now three years old) was born from the second pregnancy, but is a sickly child. He experiences nightmares and says he sees a human or spirit-like figure which tells him he will pay for his father's burning its (the spirit's) stuff. Netsai took Zvitendo to a medicine person. The medicinal roots prescribed by the medicine person appeared to have a beneficial effect on Zvitendo, but Nhamo found the roots and threw them away. The illness has strained Nhamo's relationship with his wife, extended family and the church. Every time Nhamo feels better the son gets worse physically. The pastor is the only person with whom Nhamo will discuss these concerns.

This summarized case is an example of the problem this book addresses as upper middle class urban Shona Christians struggle between two conflicting sets of religious and cultural values. The Shona people, especially upper middle class Shonas living in cities, are at a crossroads as they feel they must choose between Shona traditional religio-culture and Western Christian cultures.

This book focuses on the contemporary urban Shona people, particularly on the upper middle class Shona. I argue that the contemporary urban Shona context requires new and relevant paradigms in pastoral theology of care to address problems experienced by those living in such a context. As will be argued in greater detail, a Shona pastoral caregiver needs to have an integrative consciousness in order to relevantly address the problems of the modern day urban Shona Christians. This chapter serves as an introduction to this book and also presents the purpose and problem this book addresses.

---

3 A horn filled with blood (gona) can symbolize an evil force or something used to combat evil or to prevent evil from attacking one or one's family.

The Problem

From the time when Zimbabwe was colonized as Rhodesia (1890), fears arose among the Shona people concerning the impact of colonization on their freedom, culture, and religious tradition. The British colonization of Zimbabwe was not achieved without resistance. Native indignation (from both Shona and Ndebele people) at the colonization of Zimbabwe resulted in rebellions in 1896 to1897, formation of political parties, and ultimately a war of liberation (1965-1979) which led to independence in 1980. Mungazi, a Shona historian, notes:

> The first two administrators of colonial Zimbabwe [Rhodesia], Leander Starr Jameson (from September 10, 1890 to April, 1896), and Earl Grey (from April 2, 1896 to December 4, 1898), shared the views of their mentor and financier Cecil John Rhodes (1853-1901), who expressed his belief in the first stage of colonizing all of Africa and bringing it under British rule for at least a thousand years. But it was the rest of the colonial officials. . .from William Milton, who served from December 5, 1898 to October 31, 1914, to Ian Smith, who served from April 1,1964 to March 3, 1979. . .who lived and functioned by the Victorian views of the Africans and thereby set the two racial groups on a collision course.[4]

The Victorian view or belief held that Europeans were superior to Africans and Africans were less human than the Europeans. The Europeans were to be lords over the Africans.[5]

Muphree, a Methodist missionary and scholar who taught at what was known as the University of Rhodesia, quotes an anonymous statement he says was made in London on February, 17,1962, by someone who was then the leader of the largest nationalist party from Zimbabwe:

> "We do not want to be Europeans; we want to be Africans. The Whites thought that they could destroy our African culture, but they failed; it has only gone underground. It is still there, and we shall resurrect it. We shall take from the

---

4 Dickson A. Mungazi, *Colonial Policy and Conflict in Zimbabwe: A Study of Cultures in Collision, 1890-1979* (New York: Crane Russak, Taylor and Francis Group, 1992), xx.

5 Ibid., 27.

> European culture that which can help us, but we shall blend it with African culture, and the end result will be *African*."[6]

In today's urban Shona context, it appears that the indigenous culture has not been fully "resurrected," but is going deeper "underground," as the present generations are becoming more and more Westernized. Among scholars of African literature, African cultural studies, and some of the older generations, there is a fear that the Shona culture is disappearing. The expressed fear by the leaders in 1962 is increasingly becoming a reality; the blending for which the older generation had hoped seems to be occurring at the expense of the Shona culture. The younger generation is taking more from the European foreign culture than from the indigenous Shona culture. As will be expounded later, becoming caught between the Western and Shona traditional cultures creates confusion for the younger generation with regard to what it means to be a Shona, resulting in lack of clarity in terms of personal identity.

Gelfand, a medical doctor and professor from the former University of Rhodesia, illustrated this confusion as he researched and wrote extensively on the culture and religion of the Shona people. In a chapter entitled, "The Urban Shona and the Degree of Change," based on a survey conducted in 1970 in the capital city of then Salisbury (now Harare), Gelfand focused on questions related to blood relations, and how modernization impacted such relations. Gelfand asked his respondents about the general impact of modernization on traditional life and culture, especially with regard to those who had moved from rural areas and who were now living in the cities. After receiving feedback from colleagues about some of the weaknesses of his survey, Gelfand reworked the questions and repeated the survey. The following is Gelfand's conclusion from his 1971 survey:

> There is no denying that Western culture has changed the lives of the Shona people. . .There is probably no phase of their lives that has not been affected by the advent of the European. It is often said that they are fast losing their cultural habits and that in the not too distant future, perhaps in a few decades, they will become like the American Negroes [African-Americans] who have long forgotten most of their African forbears. . .If an observer were to enter the home of a

---

6 Marshall W. Muphree, *Christianity and the Shona* (New York: Humanities Press Inc., 1969), 13.

> married family and look around he might easily come to the conclusion that the people are fast becoming Westernized.[7]

Gelfand, whose survey occurred almost thirty years ago, found that the impact of the Western influence was apparent in the lives of the Shona people. The changes are taking place all over the country, but the greatest impact is readily evident in the cities. In this book, this author is not going to address the changes brought about by Westernization all over Zimbabwe, but will focus instead on the contemporary urban Shona context.

The tension from changes taking place in the lives of the Shona seems to be increasing, particularly in the urban areas. A Zimbabwean daily newspaper, *The Herald*, published the following article illustrating the problems some contemporary urban Shonas are facing:

> Children of some indigenous Black people in Zimbabwe are in danger of losing their mother language and culture. The crisis has reached a point where some school authorities discourage their students from speaking vernacular languages such as Shona and Ndebele, insisting on English, the language of British settlers who colonized Zimbabwe in 1890.
>
> Some parents also forbid their children from using the vernacular language in their homes, demanding English as the household language, 16 years into independence and Black majority rule. According to Dr. John Rwambiwa, a University Zimbabwean Lecturer in Education, some Zimbabweans wrongly equate intelligence with the ability to speak English well. . .To reverse the disturbing trend, a Shona Language committee was launched recently to spearhead the cultural value of Shona. . .The original committee lapsed in 1985, paving the way for Shona to fade mainly among the youths while the use of too much English crept in.[8]

This statement's content and tone clearly show that the changes affecting the young generation are detrimental to the traditional knowledge and understanding of the indigenous culture. Two months later, the same newspaper, in its Sunday edition, had an article quoting opinions of local

---

7 Michael Gelfand, *The Genuine Shona, Survival Values of an African Culture* (Gweru: Mambo Press, 1992), 180-182.

8 Chemist Mafuba, "Children Risk Losing Mother Tongue, Culture," *The Herald*, (Harare) 17 June 1996, 22. This quotation is not translated; it is a direct quote from the newspaper.

Shona writers and other scholars on issues of identity and culture in contemporary Zimbabwe:

> There are fears that Zimbabwean culture is dying and not much is being done to preserve it. . ."Modernity, progress, comfort are good but what becomes of our identity?" asks Chimanikire. . .And as long as English remains the gateway to anything in Zimbabwe, parents are justified for not encouraging their children to speak or learn local languages. . .When the kids go to school or creche [pre-school], the requirements topping the selection criteria is *kune varungu here /kuno taurwa chirungu here?* (Are there Whites and is English the medium of communication?). "It is enough that Shona is forbidden at the school or creche." Munjeri says local languages are on the verge of extinction. . .Chenjerai also asked why local writers were read more outside the borders, and why Zimbabwe's education system remained colonially biased with teachings of Shakespeare. "Who, among our learned people, can quote my works or Charles Mungoshi's off the cuff, over dinner or drink? But how many lines of Shakespeare are floating in our minds right now? Does that give us a hint as to the faulty nature of our education system? A system which approximates to teaching us self-hate," said Hove.[9]

Self-hate, personal and cultural identity confusion, and loss of the traditional language of self expression are problems and key themes to which the above articles point and with which the contemporary Zimbabwean Shona urban population must contend. Because language and culture are so intimately connected, with the extinction of a language comes the extinction of a culture and a people's identity. Identity and culture are passed on mainly through communication and/or language. This argument about how language, culture, and identity influence one another will be elucidated in the second chapter.

Lambo, a former Deputy Director-General of the World Health Organization in Geneva, stated that the general African social emotional and economic situation exacerbates the problem of personal identity conflict:

> Within our societies there are presently the following symptoms: collision (and fusion in some cases) of two or more cultures; the disrupting effects of industrialization; the emotional and social insecurity and isolation of the individual who is transplanted from the rural to the urban environment; the

---

9 Millie Phiri, "Much has to be Done to Save our Culture," *The Sunday Mail,* (Harare) 25 August 1996, C1.

> assumption of new roles, for example by young politicians, with consequent erosion of authority of the traditional elders. All this is coupled with the accompanying switch in moral and social values in the process of shedding off tribal life, thereby creating what may be termed existential frustration and existential vacuum. But there can be little doubt, unfortunately, that the cultural mingling and imposed or forced acceptance found in Africa now and in the past can often be adverse to painless evolution and have brought in their train psychopathological upheavals and severe conflicts, only too familiar to some of us.[10]

Although Lambo is addressing the general African situation, and as also evidenced by the preceding newspaper quotations, this is also true of the Zimbabwean context. In the contemporary urban Shona Christian context, at least two generations struggle, caught between the Western and the traditional cultures. The "upheavals and severe conflicts," to which Lambo refers, result in personal identity conflicts brought about by the clash between Westernization and the traditional African cultures. Further, as Lambo notes, the problem of living in two or more cultures creates an "existential frustration" and "existential vacuum" in the lives of the Shonas.

Shona adults who live in the cities may hold the values of the traditional culture, while at the same time find themselves having to exist at work as a Westerner, eight hours of the day. The result is internal incongruence. The same applies to many school children in that they spend close to the same amount of time within an educational system which is European or Western oriented in its teaching and modeling. The children then return to homes which may be divided on whether or not to enforce traditional value systems. At home, both adults and children are exposed to Western culture through the medium of television and radio, further blurring the cultural values. It is general knowledge in Zimbabwe that the younger generation listeners' most popular radio station (Radio Three) plays almost no Shona songs. Its production is probably ninety-eight percent English language, predominately playing music such as Rap, R&B, and other popular music from the West.

10 T. Adeoye Lambo, "Mental Health of Man in Africa," *African Affairs* 80 (April,1981): 278.

Hybridity and Consciousness

Young, an author and professor from England, asserts that existence in a context of living between two opposing cultures produces "hybridity" in terms of culture and identity.[11] Young traces the use of the word hybridity from a cultural theorist perspective. He begins with a study of the term, noting it was originally used in biology to discuss the cross-breeding of animals. Later, the word was used in reference to the creation of a new language by mixing two distinct languages. Today, it is being appropriated to describe cultural contexts where two different cultural systems, a traditional and a foreign system, exist without either of the cultures eradicating the other, thereby producing a hybrid culture. In other words, a hybrid is one which is a "half-breed" of the two opposing cultures or religious values.

To Mwikamba, a Catholic priest and lecturer in the Department of Religious Studies at Nairobi University, definition of the modern African person parallels the concept of hybridity, especially among the upper middle class urban Shona Christians:

> The African of today is a 'modern person' and feels the full impact, if not the blast, of 'modern civilization,' and its consequences.
>
> Many Africans are torn apart: in some sense, they are 'falling apart.' The sense of being 'double,' 'a split personality,' of being 'half,' is felt by many Africans, who are influenced by dualities: 'two cultures,' 'two morals,' 'two value-systems' and 'two world-views': the African and the Western.[12]

What Mwikamba is describing there is similar to hybridity (in the form of naive consciousness, explained below), which becomes dangerous in terms of one's identity when one is caught between two opposing cultural value systems.

Hybridity impacts people differently, creating at least two different levels of consciousness. Both the upper middle class urban Shona people

---

11 Robert J. C. Young, *Colonial Desire* (London & New York: Routledge, 1995), 44ff.

12 Constantine M. Mwikamba, "A Search for an African Identity," *AFER-African Ecclesial Review* 31 (February, 1989): 92.

and the pastoral caregivers experience hybridity in their everyday lives. However, the pastoral caregiver, in this urban context, must be a different type of hybrid from the parishioner, or possess a different level of consciousness from that of the parishioners, to be effective. The word consciousness is used in terms of an awareness.[13]

Dooyeweerd, who was Professor of Philosophy of Law at Free University of Amsterdam, wrote about two levels of consciousness, calling them "naive consciousness" and "critical consciousness." He notes that naive consciousness is similar to naive experience:

> . . .naive experience is exclusively concerned with the typical total structures of individuality and does not explicitly distinguish aspects,. . .this datum [of naive experience] must be converted by philosophy into fundamental problem; it should analyze the typical structures of individuality which also constitute a philosophic problem; modern science breaks up the naive concept of a thing in order to gain knowledge of the functional coherence of the phenomena within special modal aspect. . .[14]

Even though Dooyeweerd is writing about philosophical theories and natural sciences, what he is addressing could be applied to everyday life. His above cited "naive consciousness" is observed when people approach situations uncritically or without any analysis or objectivity.

The second approach, a different level of consciousness, uses critical consciousness or analysis. Dooyeweerd notes:

> . . .common experience is called naive and at the same time rooted in an epistemological theory to be refuted by the "critical" analysis of knowledge, our

---

13 The word consciousness in this book means a mental or cognitive awareness, being knowledgeable, informed or enlightened about something or processes. Consciouness is similar to the notion of conscientization by Freire which is the ability to perceive and clarify oppressive situations critically, Paulo Freire, *Pedagogy of the Oppressed*, trans. Myra Bergman Ramos (New York: Continuum, 1983), 20. This is different from the psychodynamic use of the word which refers to emotional processes where something needs to move from the repressed subconscious to consciousness.

14 Herman Dooyeweerd, *A New Critique of Theoretical Thought*, vol. iv. (Philadelphia: The Presbyterian and Reformed Publishing Co., 1969), 164.

> consciousness in the naive attitude is systaltic; the refutation of naive experience is based on the unreliability of sensory perception as to "objective" reality. . .[15]

In other words, what Dooyeweerd is saying above is that naive consciousness is not always reliable, and that life situations have to be approached at a level of critical consciousness. I am arguing, in this book, that even in everyday practical situations, critical consciousness is required to work with people in any pastoral care setting among the urban Shona. This hybrid (based in critical consciousness) way of functioning allows the caregiver the ability to respond to parishioners from an integrative perspective. Such a perspective allows the trained pastoral caregiver the ability to critically analyze situations of care brought to their attention and flexibility in approach, method and world-view.

There is also the question of the difference between an integrative consciousness (critical consciousness) and a hybrid consciousness of the form of naive consciousness. A hybrid of the naive consciousness type, in this book, refers to the consciousness of one who does not really know who one is, in terms of religious or cultural identity. In other words, a hybrid with a naive consciousness is a person who is in a state of flux. A person with a naive consciousness often has identity confusion; s/he questions whether s/he is Shona or Western in terms of personality. The same person may also question whether s/he is Christian or an African traditionalist in his/her religious values and practices.

On the other hand, a person with an integrative consciousness (critical consciousness) is aware of the struggles involved in the process of this identity confusion. The pastoral caregiver with an integrative consciousness is trained and educated in a method of analysis that utilizes a critical approach. Such a pastoral person has the ability to analyze situations beyond the presenting problem. In this book integrative consciousness and critical consciousness will be used to refer to the same phenomenon. Critical consciousness requires hermeneutical skills with which to analyze situations that are influenced by two cultures and two religious world-views, and to avoid naive value judgments which can impede providing

---

15 Ibid., 165.

adequate care. The term integrative consciousness is used interchangeably with critical consciousness in this book.

In addition, a caregiver with a critical consciousness has been trained to understand the identity confusion, may have experienced the identity confusion, and/or has resolved it for one's personal self or identity. To give a simple example, each person who is a pastoral caregiver is not free of problems in his/her life. Pastoral caregivers experience life in many similar ways as those to whom they provide care. It is, however, hoped that the pastoral caregivers' training enhances their problem solving skills to enable them to help others. The proposition here is that a pastoral caregiver has gone through the training, has acquired skills to help those still going through the crisis of hybridity and, as a result, has developed an integrative consciousness. This writer is arguing that a pastoral caregiver with an integrative consciousness becomes a "bridge to understanding" the cultural, personal, and religious identity confusions of the careseekers and parishioners.

I am positing that, in the urban Shona context, most of the upper middle class Christian people live at the level of naive consciousness due to urban pressures, bi-culturalism, bi-religiousness, or the need to succeed economically (as will be explored later).[16] Those experiencing identity confusion are experiencing naive consciousness. The trained pastoral caregiver practices at a level of critical consciousness enabling him/her to help parishioners operating at a hybrid of naive consciousness level. The level of consciousness of upper middle class urban Shona people, who seek help from pastoral caregivers because of identity confusion, is of naive consciousness and is problematic. The problems produced by this type of hybridity of naive consciousness are many. The illustrative case of Nhamo and Netsai indicate the experiences of hybridity experienced by most upper middle class urban Shona Christians.

16 Bi-culturalism means one finds himself or herself caught between the tension of two opposing cultures. There are times the person may culturally move back and forth in utilizing the cultural values, and other times they may simultaneously mix the cultural values. Bi-religiousness, however, is a bit more restrictive, since the traditional Shona religion was condemned as paganistic. Bi-religiouness means one is caught between the tension of two contradictory religions. There is no room given to move back and forth freely in utilizing the religious values.

As a result of hybridity of the naive consciousness type, one's way of existence is sometimes compromised in a struggle for one's survival. The Shona traditional culture is communal, while the Western culture is individualistic. For example, with the pressure of the colonizing culture to succeed economically, one may choose to sever one's extended family relationships in order to become successful (as defined by the foreign culture). This choice reflects the conflict between the individual and the communal way the Shonas live their lives. Ignoring traditional family and community cultural values causes great anxiety. The anxiety is an outgrowth of guilt about purposely ignoring communal values traditionally held dear (e.g., devaluing extended family relations in order to favor material gains). In the Shona context, one's relationships are valued over material things; to do otherwise is a source of immense guilt, only correctable by righting and reconciling the severed relationships.

Hybridity of the naive consciousness type can also result in one believing in, and placing more worth on, Western values than the traditional Shona cultural values. Many members of the young urban generation may view the Shona traditional values as "an ancient and uncivilized" way of life, while the modern Western way of life is seen as "the civilized way of life." Mwikamba notes:

> Some of the Africans are running from themselves and from their traditional past. This has been caused by the rapid internalization of some aspects of Western culture. Many Africans today believe that the Western value system and world-view are of universal validity, which, as such, must be applicable also to Africa. Many believe that Africans can 'catch up,' and be like people of the 'developed' countries. Such mental enslavement is the worst side-effect of colonialism and of the unculturated missionary activity.[17]

When the modern Western ways fail to provide answers, self-conflict erupts. A person who embraces solely modern values can no longer find answers through the so-called "uncivilized" means, due to pride in an internalized colonial mentality which promotes the attitude that Western values are always superior to those of the traditional Shona values. The above point, concerning the conflict of traditional versus Western values,

---

17 Constantine M. Mwikamba, "A search for an African Identity," *AFER -African Ecclesial Review* 31 (February, 1989): 95.

is explored further in the third chapter, and illustrated in the case studies herein.

Hybridity and Religious Perspective. Naive consciousness is also a problem when viewed from a religious perspective. Religiously, the contemporary urban Shona find themselves struggling with issues of Christianity versus the traditional Shona religion. There are many religious denominations from which the urban Shona Christians can choose. The religious aspect of this book focuses mainly on those contemporary urban Shona Christians who belong to the "mainline" churches in Zimbabwe, specifically the United Methodist church. In Africa, the term "mainline churches" refers to the Catholic and Protestant denominations.

The other churches in Zimbabwe are Independent churches. These are often indigenous churches founded and led by the local African people. I am of the opinion that Independent churches have done and continue to do a better job of blending the African traditional religion with Christianity without creating a dilemma or conflict for their members.[18] Bishop Hatendi, a Shona bishop of the Anglican church in Zimbabwe, supports the idea that most Independent churches are doing a better job of blending traditional and Western religions:

> . . .Shona indigenous Churches are sympathetic and accommodating. They do not regard being a Shona or marrying like a Shona as contrary to the known will of God. While the white-led churches would like to see the Shona 'apologize' for being what he is, the black-led Churches teach that he has no apology to make as regards his culture but to believe in the saving grace of Christ.[19]

---

18 There are a variety of these churches; some are very fundamentalistic in their practices of Christianity and the others are very accommodative of the traditional Shona religion and culture. This author's reference here to Independent churches refers to those which are accommodative of, and those which try to blend Western Christianity with the traditional Shona religion and culture.

19 R. P. Hatendi, "Shona Marriage and the Christian Churches," in A. J. Dachs ed., *Christianity South of the Zambezi*, vol. 1, (Gweru: Mambo Press, 1973), 147. This notion of mainline churches degrading the Independent churches is a topic which warrants its own attention altogether.

Even though Hatendi (who is from the mainline churches) states the above, arguments such as his have not protected the African Independent churches from being criticized as not truly Christian. Daneel, a scholar who has researched and written extensively on Independent churches in Zimbabwe and in Africa in general, says the following about the attitude of mainline churches toward Independent churches in Zimbabwe: "They are often referred to as sectarian, separatist, heretical or nativistic movements. Many of them undoubtedly reveal strong syncretistic tendencies. . ."[20] The term "syncretistic tendencies" refers to the efforts by the Independent churches to blend Western Christianity with traditional Shona religious values. I am not opposed to the efforts of the Independent churches in blending Western Christianity and traditional Shona religion, but do not advocate reclaiming all of the African traditional religious values without applying a critical analysis of the contemplated necessity of blending each particular ritual. I advocate an effort to reclaim and integrate those rituals and values not contrary to the Western Christian teachings which are utilized in the urban Shona churches today. Scholars such as Hatendi and Daneel have already written extensively on the subject of the work of Independent churches in Africa. Hence, this book will not pursue that debate, but will leave it to others.

Along with personal identity confusion comes confusion about religious identity. One of the main causes of religious identity conflict occurs when people feel caught between traditional Shona religious practices (condemned as paganistic by the missionaries) and Western Christian religious values. Whidborne, who has written on religion in Southern Africa, and more specifically on Zimbabwe, says this about the Shona's experience of religious conflict:

> . . .the difficulties facing the Shona Christians of balancing the beliefs and practices preached by the missionaries against the more traditional Shona values are often chronic. When a man has an essential function in a traditional ritual he is expected to fulfill it regardless of whether he belongs to some Christian church. The influence of the Shona community has seen many Christians surreptitiously

20 M. L. Daneel, "The Growth and Significance of Shona Independent Churches," in M. F. C. Bourdillon ed., *Christianity south of the Zambezi*, vol. 2, (Gweru: Mambo Press, 1977), 177.

> accede to the demands of the society against the regulations of the Church. . . converts carried their traditional beliefs to their new faith so that 'the juxtaposition of the two religious systems has not resulted in, nor necessitated, a categorical rejection of either in its totality.'[21]

Whidborne is suggesting that the missionaries created this "chronic" situation for the Shonas by never taking time to examine the similarities between the two religions. Instead, the traditional religion was labeled paganistic by missionaries, thereby creating problems for those who converted to Christianity, yet still honored Shona traditional rituals and practices. Bishop Hatendi affirms this missionary attitude toward Shona religion and customs:

> The missionary's attitude to Shona customs and tradition is often determined by his preconceived image of the Shona. The attitude generally adopted may be to label everything Shona 'heathen' or 'pagan.' Since heathendom and Christendom are ruled by the Devil and Christ respectively, they are incompatible. It is the missionary's objective to substitute heathen faith and practice with Christian faith and practice. It means declaring war on Shona culture. For the missionary 'conversion' means turning away from the Shona culture and accepting the Western way of life. Faith in Jesus as Savior comes last.[22]

This negative missionary attitude toward the Shona culture, religion, and customs, planted in most converts' minds in the mainline churches, has not died away; in fact, it is the basis of the religious values of most of the mainline Christian churches today in Africa, and specifically in the United Methodist church in Zimbabwe.

In the traditional Shona way of life, religion is closely intertwined with culture. Inadequate knowledge of the indigenous language, culture, and religion of the Shonas develops a breeding ground for personal and religious identity confusion among the urban Shona people. The problem of hybridity in culture and religion surfaces clearly in the contemporary urban Shona context when Christians seek pastoral care on issues which make them feel they must choose between the traditional Shona and the

---

21 Vicki Whidborne, "Africanization of Christianity in Zimbabwe," *Religion in Southern Africa* 4 (Jan, 1993): 33.

22 R. P. Hatendi, "Shona Marriage and the Christian Churches," in J. A. Dachs ed., *Christianity South of the Zambezi*, vol. 1, (Gweru: Mambo Press, 1973), 145-146.

Western culture and between Western Christianity and traditional Shona religion.

Pastoral Theology and Care in non-Western Contexts. This book, in the field of pastoral care, focuses on pastoral care in non-Western contexts, specifically the urban contemporary Shona Christian context. Traditionally, pastoral theology and care, as practiced in the West, has given scant attention to the historical, traditional religious, and cultural contexts of non-Western settings. Only recently has attention turned toward cross-cultural issues in pastoral theology and care. Clinebell, a North American pastoral counselor, recognizes this when he says:

> Pastoral care must liberate itself from its dominant middle class, white, male orientation and become more inclusive in its understanding, concerns and methods. It must become transcultural in its perspective, open to learning new ways of caring from and for the poor and powerless, ethnic minorities, women and those in non-Western cultures. On a shrinking planet, our circle of consciousness, conscience, and caring must become global.[23]

Augsburger, another North American pastoral theologian, makes a comparable argument about pastoral care in non-Western contexts when he argues that people of non-Western cultures encounter pastoral care problems which are sometimes similar to those in the West, but which need to be solved in culturally appropriate ways.[24] Direct transference of Western theories to non-Western peoples, without consideration of the indigenous cultural and religious context, is inappropriate and harmful. For pastors who will serve in the Shona context, education and training in pastoral theology and care must incorporate the totality of life, culture, and world-views of the people who are served.

Similarly, a compilation of papers from the Pan-African Conference of Third World Theologians emphasizes that, in order to speak to the needs and daily struggles of the African people, there is a need for a new

---

23 Howard Clinebell, *Basic Types of Pastoral Care and Counseling* (Nashville: Abingdon, 1984), 27.

24 David Augsburger, *Pastoral Counseling Across Cultures* (Philadelphia: Westminster Press, 1986).

theology, along with a new theological method applied by Africans in the African context.[25] This theology must not get its definition solely from Western theologies, but must be created out of the African people's conditions. Those who have written from the Zairian, Ghanian, Kenyan, South African, and other African contexts have aired the same sentiments about the importance of cultural, historical, traditional religious values for non-Western contexts in dealing with issues of pastoral theology and care.[26] An important component of such a theological development must address how colonization and Westernization changed - or continues to change - communal interpersonal relations, social structures, and personal identity due to the differences in world-views between traditional Shona religio-culture and Western Christianity and culture.[27] This book looks specifically at how colonization impacts pastoral theology of care. While there is literature about education and counseling psychology, there is none that specifically addresses a pastoral theology of care for the Shona context.[28] The transition taking place, in the culture and religion of the Shona, requires new literature to address the urban Shona context. It is this deficiency in the Shona context which this book intends to address.

---

25 S. Appiah-Kubi & S. Torres, eds., *African Theology En Route* (New York: Peter Lang, 1989).

26 See authors such as Gerald Hawkes, "The Relationship Between Theology and Practice in South African Pastoral Theology," in Masamba ma Mpolo ed., *Pastoral Care and Counselling in Africa Today* (New York: Peter Lang, 1991); Emmauel Y. Lartey, *Pastoral Counselling in Inter-cultural Perspective: A Study of Some African (Ghanaian) and Anglo-American Views on Human Existence and Counselling* (New York: Peter Lang, 1987); Masamba ma Mpolo, ed., *The Risk of Growth: Counselling & Pastoral Theology in the African Context* (Nigeria: Daystar Press, 1985); David W. Waruta, ed., *Caring and Sharing: Pastoral Counselling in the African Perspective* (Nairobi: Kenya, Act Print Ltd., 1995).

27 Communal interpersonal relations implies one gets a sense of belonging and self from existing in good relationship with other humans, creatures, God, Spirit world, living dead-ancestors, and the yet unborn.

28 See Fidelis Chikara and R. S. Manley, "Psychiatry in Zimbabwe," *Hospital & Community Psychiatry* 42 (9 Sept, 1991): 943; Elias Mpofu, "Exploring the Self-Concept in an African Culture," *Journal of Genetic Psychology* 155 (Sept,1994): 341-354.

One's historical (and at times geographical) context influences theology, understanding, and internalization of God images, and religious understanding of self in relationship to others, in addition to ways with which to relate to the external world. It is essential for a pastor to understand the changes which have affected the Shona people before attempting to address any issues pertaining to pastoral theology and care; one's history influences one's theological standpoint, one's self-understanding and one's approach to pastoral theology, and care.

Indigenous pastoral caregivers must take caution not to impose their own internalized colonial bondage or the mistaken notion that Western individualistic theories are superior to traditional ones found in non-Western situations. Relatedly, caregivers must not impose solely traditional methods of providing care, since the Shona context (having been under the influence of other external forces such as Western Christianity) has changed in and of itself.

Pastoral caregivers must recognize that they work in an urban Shona context in which religious, personal, and cultural identity are fragmented due to bi-religious and bi-cultural experiences of the urban contemporary Shona Christians.[29] The contemporary urban Shonas find themselves existing in a bi-cultural and bi-religious context: living in tension between Shona and Western cultures, as well as between African traditional religion and Western Christianity. In urban settings, the force of economics and urban planning results in encouraging the Shonas, who are usually communally oriented people, to live individualistic lives which are contrary to their traditional religio-culture.

Living in a bi-cultural and bi-religious context predisposes one to conflictual identities. How did colonization, Christianity and Westernization greatly impact traditional pastoral care by changing communal interpersonal relations? How can pastoral care be made effective and relevant to the contemporary urban Shona who have such bi-cultural and bi-religious experiences?

---

29 The urban Shona Christians are those who have made the city their home and may occasionally go to the rural areas (villages) to visit. The older people (urban) are often knowledgeable about the traditional religion and culture, while the youth in this urban context may not be well informed about the traditional Shona religion and culture.

This book in the field of pastoral theology and care focuses on the Shona people, with a goal to elucidate missing pieces from traditional Shona religious culture in order to develop a Shona pastoral theology of care. Specifically, it addresses issues of pastoral theology relevant to the contemporary urban upper middle class Shona Christians. A Shona pastoral theology of care refers to a pastoral theology coming out of a Shona context; it is informed by the practical situations Shona pastors must address. As a pastoral theology, it is interdisciplinary as it integrates African traditional religion, culture, African theology, Christianity, and psychology.[30] A pastoral theology of care is one which informs, directs, and influences how one provides pastoral care. As such, pastoral theology is concerned with providing a theory which informs the practice of pastoral care.[31] Prior to colonization, pastoral theology and care were present in the traditional Shona context, even though they were not articulated or denoted as such.[32] ma Mpolo notes, from a historical perspective, the direction of pastoral care in Africa:

> The African pastoral care movement has been developing three major orientations: the first is rooted in Western theories, seeking to describe pastoral care in European patterns of pastoral theology (Tjega, 1971; Nomenyo, 1971). The second is purely descriptive and academic interpretation of health and healing using African patterns of thought and traditional therapies (Mwene-Batende, 1981). The third approach attempts to integrate both systems and uses African

---

30 As much as I agree with Martin that African cultural and religious contexts are diverse and plural, when the word "African" is used it is encompassing of the Shona. Denis C. Martin, "Out of Africa! Should we be Done with Africanism," in *The Surreptitious Speech, Presence Africaine and the Politic of Otherness 1947-1987* (Chicago & London: University of Chicago, 1992), 47-48.

31 T. W. Jennings, "Pastoral Theological Methodology," Rodney Hunter, ed., *Dictionary of Pastoral Care and Counseling* (Nashville: Abingdon, 1990), 862-864.

32 ma Mpolo argues that pastoral care, counseling, and psychiatry systems in the Western sense are new in the African context, but these systems have always been aspects of the indigenous African religion and medical system. Masamba ma Mpolo, "Perspectives on African Pastoral Counseling," *The Risk of Growth: Counseling and Pastoral Theology in the African Context* (Nigeria: Daystar Press, 1985), 1.

> cultures, biblical theology, and Western psychodynamically oriented psychotherapy and proposes pastoral implications for the churches.[33]

I find myself in the third category of integration, in terms of both theories and approaches in providing pastoral care in the urban Shona Christian context. In addition to the above approaches, ma Mpolo recommends "further theoretical and practical research," for the development of a pastoral care that is contextual to Africa, utilizing three dynamics:

> (1) the importance of understanding the parishioner's or client's world-view; (2) the importance of incorporating cultural concepts of illness and health into the therapeutic process; (3) the necessity of inserting insight-oriented approaches into the pastoral care and therapeutic process in order to promote emotional release or catharsis, personality growth, and an awareness of one's identity in relation to that of the group.[34]

ma Mpolo's recommendation for further research and development of theories relevant for Africa, and in this case for the urban Shona context, is the goal of this book. Central to this book are the recommendations stated earlier by ma Mpolo to: "understand the parishioner's world-view. . .," "incorporating the cultural concepts of illness and health," and "to promote . . . personality growth and an awareness of one's identity in relation to that of the group."

Given some of the negative impact which colonization, Christianity, and Westernization had on the Shonas, it is of great importance that caregivers evaluate their theories and pastoral theological standpoints in light of the contemporary urban Shona context before trying to provide effective pastoral care to seekers of such care. This requires that pastors be equipped with a new pastoral theological and psychodynamic understanding of integrative consciousness. "Integrative consciousness" means that a pastor must possess an awareness of, knowledge of, or easily comprehend both the Shona and the Western world-views, as well as the

---

33 Masamba ma Mpolo, "African Pastoral Care Movement," in Rodney J. Hunter ed., *Dictionary of Pastoral Care and Counseling* (Nashville: Abingdon, 1990), 12.

34 Ibid.

blending and integration of aspects of Shona and Western world-views in personal or religious identity formation and/or in providing care.

The urban setting of bi-cultural and bi-religious lives predisposes Shona Christians to experience anxiety, which tends to intensify in times of crisis. This anxiety forces some of the Shonas to seek the help of the pastor, since in urban areas the village setting of aunts, uncles, and grandparents from whom to seek counsel no longer exists. With an integrative consciousness, the caregiver can better assist those with dysfunctional personal and religious interpersonal relations which result from life in bi-religious and bi-cultural contexts. As aforementioned, integrative consciousness is equated with the critical consciousness, while those experiencing identity confusion are experiencing naive consciousness. The trained pastoral caregiver practices at a level of critical consciousness, enabling him/her to help parishioners operating at a hybrid level of naive consciousness.

The focus of this book is on identity conflict caused by changes due to historic events which took place in the Shona context, mainly the advent of colonization and the introduction of Christianity by the missionaries. However, this book also has implications for the general African population. Chapter Two presents a synopsis of traditional Shona religious culture and a brief history of the coming of Western Christianity, colonization, and its impact on contemporary Zimbabwe. Chapter Three presents Sullivan's theory of personal identity, interpersonal relations, and anxiety. From the psychodynamic perspective, the work of Sullivan provides insights into personal identity formation. Sullivan is not the only theorist who addresses the importance of community in one's identity formation; Erikson and Mead, for example, argue in similar ways.[35] However, Sullivan uses clinical work to show how dysfunctional interpersonal relations are related to anxiety. The argument is that Sullivan's theory gives insight into the urban Shonas' experience; he postulates that anxiety is a result of dysfunctional interpersonal relations.

---

35 Erik E. H. Erikson, *Identity and The life Cycle* (New York: International University Press: 1959); George H. Mead, *Mind, Self and Society* (Chicago: University of Chicago Press, 1934); Harry. S. Sullivan, *Interpersonal Theory of Psychiatry* (New York: W. W. W. Norton & Co., 1972).

In addition, the third chapter briefly outlines Shona traditional personal identity development and discusses how colonization and Westernization have changed the personal identity development for the contemporary urban Shona person.

Chapter Four presents examples of traditional Shona relational theology and changes which have taken place due to the advent of Christianity. The goal of the chapter is an attempt to demonstrate that communal interpersonal relations between God, humans, and nature, in the traditional Shona society, are predicated on religion. This chapter highlights aspects of relational theology based on the traditional Shona religion, which can be utilized by the contemporary urban Shona pastoral caregiver.

Chapter Five is a presentation and analysis of composite case studies demonstrating how issues of dysfunctional interpersonal relationships cause identity confusion, resulting in psychological and religious anxiety for the contemporary Shonas Christians. Some suggestions for pastoral responses which might be relevant to the urban contemporary Shona context are also presented in the analysis.

Chapter Six is the conclusion. It lays out some implications for pastoral theology of care in the education and training of pastoral caregivers for the Shona context specifically, and for the field of pastoral theology and care in general. It presents some examples of rituals and religious values needed to be incorporated in the urban Shona Christian churches, and in the training of its pastors.

CHAPTER TWO

Traditional Shona Religio-culture, Colonization and Western Christianity

This chapter gives a brief historical background of the Shona people's traditional religion and culture, social structures, and life cycle and rituals. More details of the Shona traditional religious culture and identity development will be presented in Chapters Three and Four. Some of the changes that have taken place due to the advent of Western Christianity, colonization, and Westernization will be part of the discussion of this chapter. Material on post-colonial discourse will help further the discussion of the impact of colonialism and Western Christianity on the Shona. The goal of the chapter is to present a synopsis of the traditional Shona religio-culture, and to show how the advent of colonization and Western Christianity have impacted the post-colonial urban Shona Christian's religion and cultural identity.[1] Answering the following questions will also help shape and focus the discussion for this chapter. What is Shona traditional religion and culture? What are some of the Shona traditional beliefs and rituals? What are the cultural beliefs about a person's life cycle? What is the Shona traditional social system and structure?

1 Religio-cultural in this book indicates the close connection that exists between the religion and the culture of the traditional Shona people. Religion is part of one's way of life, it is part of the culture.

Traditional Shona Religio-culture: A Synopsis

Shona Traditional religion, the religion that was practiced by the Shonas before the coming of Christianity and Islam to the continent, is still practiced today in many Shona communities. The religion and culture of the Shonas is communally based. One would find that there are underlying similarities in the general communities of the Shonas, even though variations do exist from community to community. This book will not pay attention to particular regional nuances, rather it approaches the breadth of the general Shona religion and culture.[2] In the traditional Shona context, religion and culture are sometimes intertwined in ways that make it difficult to differentiate between religion and culture.

Religion is often compared to the air one breathes or is likened to one's skin: one can't take it off at any moment and one cannot live without it. Mbiti says about the African's religion: "Wherever the African is, there is his religion. . .to be without religion amounts to a self-excommunication from the entire life of the society, and African peoples do not know how to exist without religion."[3] Likewise, there are no known missionaries who have evangelized or propagated the Shona traditional religion. Among the Shonas, religion is part of one's personal human development, affecting who a person becomes. There are no known written Scriptures in the Shona religion. Shona traditional religion is passed on by oral tradition and through practice. As the common African saying suggests, "You don't teach a child about religion"; rather one learns religion through practice and observation. Just as one grows up physically and mentally, one is also believed to develop spiritually or religiously. One's life is both cultural and religious.

There are prophets and medicine people who play a central role in the traditional religion. Historically, there are three national prophets, "spirit mediums," who are said to have prophesied about the coming of the

2 For further discussion on the regional nuances see Michael Bourdillon, *The Shona Peoples* (Gweru: Mambo Press, 1991), 16ff.

3 John S. Mbiti, *African Religions and Philosophy* (New York: NY. Anchor Books, 1970), 2-3.

colonizers and missionaries: *Nehanda* (a female), and *Kaguvi and Chaminuka,* (both males). These three have attained a position of "multi-tribal" spirits. Songs sung about their prophecies during the liberation war (1965-1979) are still well remembered and sometimes sung today. The three prophesied about the coming of oppression (*udzvinyiriri)*, and about how the Europeans (*vapambepfumi)* were going to take the land by force and move the Shonas into the more barren areas.

A woman or a man can be a medicine person. In the past and in the present, many medicine people have played, and continue to play, a central role as counselors or doctors similar to psychiatrists in the West, while others act as the prophets and priests for the community. These skills are acquired either through training under another medicine person or by inheritance. It is also believed that there are some who get their training from mermaids (*njuzu*). In Zimbabwe today, some medicine people, the *N'angas*, have been incorporated into the health system of the country (ZINATHA- Zimbabwe National Traditional Healers Association). The ministry of health has found it necessary to incorporate some of the traditional practioners into the medical system of the country. On the other hand, due to the influences of Western Christianity, the church does not appear to see the necessity of honoring some of the traditional practices.

Shona Traditional Attributes and Concepts of God, and Ancestors

It is a general understanding of those who have studied the Shona religion that the Shonas believe in One Supreme Being, God (*Mwari)*. The word *Mwari*, when broken down, is *Mu-Ari*, and literally translates as "One Who Is." Daneel, who has studied and written about Independent churches, says,

> The Shona concept of the Supreme Being has never been polytheistic. The great number of names designating the Supreme Being reveal a variety of functions and the association of the divine with different phenomena of the nature rather than suggesting the existence of a number of deities. For centuries the Shona have believed in Mwari as the final authority above and behind their ancestors. . .[4]

---

4 M. L. Daneel, *Old and New in Southern Shona Independent Churches* vol.1, (The Hague: Mouton, 1971), 80-1.

As Daneel intimates, God is known by different names and attributes. The different names for God imply the type of relationship the Shonas have with God and/or how they see God relating to them. Some call God *Samasimba*, which means the One who has all the power or is the source of power, or All powerful. Others refer to God as *Nyadenga* (One who possesses or who resides in the skies/heavens), *Wokumusorosoro,* (the One who is above), *Mutangakugara*, (the One who was first in the beginning), or *Muwanikwapo* (the One who was found already in existence). *Musiki* refers to Creator or the One who created everything. As creator, God is also known as *Musikavanhu*, specifically meaning that God is the creator of humanity. Another name, *Chidzachopo,* refers to God as the One who has always been there and/or the One who is Ageless. *Dandemutande ngawi rakatandira nyika*, translates to "the web that surrounds the whole world." *Dzivaguru* means the Great Pool, with the connotation being that God supplies people with water or rains. God is also known as *Tateguru*, which means the Great Great Great Grandmother, suggesting that God is the source of life, who gave birth to all of humanity. Sometimes God is also known as *Jenandebvu* (the One with the white beard), depicting a God who resembles an old grandfather.

In the Shona religion, ancestors are of great importance; ancestors act as the mediators between God and humanity. As Mbiti says about the ancestors in all African contexts: "They have both feet in both worlds, this world and in the spiritual world."[5] Thus, when praying to God, the Shona people always prayed through the ancestors. There might be many reasons for this way to approach God. Two reasons are suggested which might be the major influences of the Shona who use these methods of praying through the ancestors.

The first reason involves the sense of respect people carry for God's name and to note God's place. There is always a hierarchy in how elders and those with greater honor and age are addressed. At the conclusion of a prayer, God's name is used, both out of respect and to acknowledge God's position at the top of the hierarchy of respect and reverence. Illustrative of this is the following prayer: *Nemi watisikachizivi*

5 Mbiti, *African Religions and Philosophy*, 25.

motisvikisirawo munamato wedu kuna SaMatenga, Mwari, Musiki wedu. This prayer translated to English says, "And you (the ancestors) we no longer remember by name, please pass our prayer of thanks or requests to the One who possesses the heavens, God our Creator."

A second reason for praying through the ancestors is closely connected to the idea of respect and honor, and the Shona understanding of death. It is believed by the traditional Shonas that a father or mother who cares for and loves his/her children must be well informed of the children's struggles and joys. In addition, parents are expected to intervene (if need be) or rejoice with the children, if there is cause for joy. The caring for and loving of one's children is not ended by death since the dead are considered to be "the living dead" or "living timeless." As they used to be informed of the struggles and joys of their children when alive, parents must continue to be informed of such pain and celebration after death. They are still living, in another form, the spiritual form, and now they can mediate for their children since they are closer to God. One would pray following the hierarchy (paternal male figures), beginning with one's father (if deceased), then the grandfather, and so forth, to the point of the name of the last person remembered in the hierarchy. At the end of the prayer, one calls upon all the other ancestors, no longer remembered by name, to take one's request to God. Bishop Hatendi notes the following,

> A person is inextricably and indissolubly one with the past, present and the future. The time concept is the observance of the collective personality. The family-group includes the dead who are revered because they are believed to be nearer the source of life; but they are never deified. They play the role of the 'go-between' as in Shona marriage and royal protocol. It is this sense that the Shona pray 'to the dead.'[6]

The Shona believe that the ancestors are present to them, but they have no power to change situations. The ancestors are dependent on God's will, taking the role of mediators. It is believed that the ancestors can speak to God on behalf of their loved ones, but they cannot change the will of God.

---

6 R. P. Hatendi, "Shona Marriage and the Christian Churches," in J. A. Dachs ed., *Christianity South of the Zambezi*, vol 1 (Gweru: Mambo Press, 1973), 146.

Since the Shona society is patriachical, the prayers are presented through the father's lineage. However, women who are dead are also ancestors and are part of the Spirit World. The spirits of both the father and the mother are expected to play the role of protecting the children and grandchildren from harmful things. These spirits can also cause illness (as a way of getting attention) if they are not remembered.

Nature, Evil Spirits and Human Beings. There are sacred places or things, such as caves, dams, mountains, and trees, but they are not worshiped. Most missionaries confused this belief with animism, thinking that Africans believed that trees have souls similar to those of human beings. While an evil spirit may reside in a tree, it is not believed to be part of the makeup of a tree. Similarly, a tree may be sacred because of events that may be performed under it, but does not have a soul as part of its essential makeup. It is believed that what affects nature affects humans, and vise-versa; therefore, a lot of emphasis is put on harmony with nature. Harmony is very important to the way of life of the Shonas and includes co-existence with nature, humanity, God, and the Spirit World.

Evil spirits exist as part of creation and can live in caves, riverbanks trees, and elsewhere. The Shona believes that it is therefore advisable that one not cut down trees at random in certain areas since these might be dwelling places for evil or for wandering spirits. For example, a wandering spirit, *shavi,* can be the spirit of a dead person who was not accorded proper burial. The only way this person's spirit can find rest is if the family accords the person proper burial, with a ceremony to send this spirit off to the Spirit World.

The traditional Shona religion holds that humans are basically born good, but they have the potential to be bad. Everything good and bad was created by God. The dualism of believing in a devil, who is the source and cause of evil, and a God who is good is not held to. There are no Shona words for 'Devil' or 'Satan.' Illustrative of the influence of the Christians' world-view are the direct translations from English *(Satani or Diabori)*. In the Shona language, an attribute, *Chirazamavi namauya,* is used in reference to God as the one who is the source of both good and bad. Murphree, in discussing the Shona beliefs in *Mwari*, talks about

Chirazamauya, "The One who provides for good and bad."[7] The attribute *Chirazamauya* (cited by Murphree) describes a God who is the giver of good, *mauya*. To make a correction on how Murphree presents the attribute, I argue that Murphree left out the word *mavi*, which means bad. The full attribute would therefore be *Chirazamavi namauya,* which means provider of good and bad.

In addition, humans, such as witches, can manipulate the forces of evil to use it against other humans. In other cases, one can become evil because the family so chooses to place an evil spirit on one. From the time of infancy, the family can give a child over (*kurasira*) to an avenging spirit, or to a dead witch's wandering spirit, which may turn the child's spirit into an evil one.

Social Systems and Structures. Shona family systems are comprised traditionally of the extended families living in the context of a village. The villages are mostly comprised of people who are related either by blood, totems, or marriage. A totem is an animal or something that symbolizes one's family, clan or group ties, or relations. A child has many uncles, fathers, mothers, sisters, and the like, through blood relations or marriage. In many cases, a child is expected to treat all these brothers or sisters (whether by relation, through marriage, or totem) with the same respect as blood brothers and sisters. Respect is given in proportion to age and responsibility; younger people are expected to respect their elders. In addition, people in general are to respect their chiefs, kings, and sometimes medicine people. In most cases, community needs are emphasized over individual needs, since individuals must bring benefit to the whole community. In traditional Shona society, communalism is more important than individualism.

Aunts and grandmothers train girls about womanhood, especially in terms of sex roles. The mother also takes the role of teaching the girls about housekeeping and raising children. The older sisters practice child rearing as they help their mothers with their younger siblings. The uncles and grandfathers teach the boys about manhood and about sex roles. The

---

7 Marshall Murphree, *Christianity and the Shona* (University of London: The Athlone Press, 1969), 49.

grandfathers, uncles, and fathers teach the boys about hunting, fishing, ploughing, building homes, and any other duties expected of men in the society. Shona traditional society was, and to a large extent remains, very patriarchal.

Interpersonal relations have a central place in the Shona religion, spiritually and socially, and in the psychological functioning of a Shona. For the traditional Shonas, disharmony in one's interpersonal relations may cause great dysfunction to one's religious, cultural, and psychological or mental stability. If any situation is suspected of bringing disharmony to the self or another, rituals are held to right the wrongs and bring harmony. However, with the coming of Christianity and colonization, there were changes in the lives of the Shonas in their personal and religious identity.

Life Cycle and Rituals. Life cycle and rituals are considered together since the rituals are involved in every transitional stage in the life cycle in African traditional religio-culture. The life cycle of the traditional Shona world is comprised of three realms: the yet unborn, (the spirit of those who have the potential to be born, whose spirits God has already created); the living, with both the spirit and body intact; and the living dead, whose bodies are dead but whose spirits live on. One's spirit, yet unborn, begins with God the Great Spirit in the Spirit World, is conceived and lives in this physical world, and then returns to the Spirit World after death. Metaphorically, death is seen as a bridge from physical life to the next life.

Even in situations not related directly to the life cycle, rituals play a key role in African people's lives. ma Mpolo, writing from a pastoral care perspective, notes how rituals from the African historical religio-cultural meaning can inform today's African society. He notes about ritual:

> Through ritual and its corresponding symbols, people tell and dramatize their stories. The pastoral counselor enters with them in telling and interpreting of such stories. . .Rituals and symbols play the role of integrating the individual in the community, provided that the community and the individual impart the same meaning to them. Rituals and symbols express the experience that the human

> being is fully human by virtue of his or her participation in a whole which transcends his/her particular existence and existential situation.[8]

The beliefs and rituals involved are sometimes contrary to Western Christian beliefs. A pastor who works with the urban Shona Christians must be aware of these contradictions to address effectively issues of anxiety that arise from the contrasts experienced by the urban Shonas in beliefs and the rituals.

There is no idea of hell in the Shona world-view. However, there is the belief that the spirit of an evil person, such as a witch, becomes restless after death. Living human beings have the power to grant, or not to grant, a dead person's spirit entrance to the Spirit World; if not accorded proper burial, or if a ritual, such as a cleansing ritual, is not performed, the deceased spirit will wander around. The cleansing ceremony, called *chenura,* allows the deceased spirit to join the Spirit World by the elder leading the ritual announcing to the Spirit World to accept the deceased spirit. Because the dead can influence the affairs of the living, they need to be remembered. In order for a positive influence to be experienced, Shonas must remember the ancestor spirits.

Shonas believe that one cannot take away a life without having consequences. The avenging spirit, *ngozi,* is believed to hound the murderer's family if reparation and rituals of reconciliation are not performed. If these rituals are not performed, the avenging spirit will not rest and will cause misfortunes, illness, and death, even to the fourth or fifth generations, until payment is given. Muphree says of the *Ngozi* spirit:

> This spirit can bring sudden retribution on those who have wronged it in life, and the procedure for placating it can involve a long and expensive process for the offender and /or his family. This process includes one of the few instances in the Budjga [a Shona sub-group] society where restitution is not made simply by the

8 ma Mpolo and Kalu, *The Risks of Growth*, 116 & 118. Other authors, even though writing from the West, see the functions of ritual in a similar way as ma Mpolo describes. For further discusion on ritual studies see Leonel L. Mitchell, *The Meaning of Ritual* (Connecticut: Morehouse-Barlow, 1988), Cathrine Bell, *Ritual Theory and Ritual Practice* (New York: Oxford University Press, 1992).

> payment of cattle or other property, but requires a long public period of public penance, known as 'Kutiza botso.'[9]

The ritual to resolve issues of a *ngozi* spirit is seen as a justice issue and as a way to restore harmony, reconciliation, and fellowship between and/or among families. A death affects the whole community, hence the involvement of the wider community in the *ngozi* ritual.

The next few paragraphs will give a synopsis the life cycle from the time of conception in a traditional Shona experience. Rituals are performed with the aid of the medicine person as soon as a woman discovers she is pregnant. *Kudzinga mamhepi,* a ritual in which the woman is given certain medicines to drink and to smear on her body, bars any evil spirits from attacking the fetus. Daneel says,

> Pregnant women are regarded as highly vulnerable. If there is the least indication or mere suspicion of an interfering spirit who wants to cause damage to a pregnant woman through 'gripping her womb,' all sorts of protective charms will be carried around the waist or upper parts of the body.[10]

A Shona woman does not announce freely that she is pregnant; to do so might provide greater opportunity for others to wish misfortune on and/or bewitch her. Traditional Shonas communally celebrate the birth of a child. The child belongs to the community from the point of birth. Protective charms are used since children are considered vulnerable to attack by evil spirits or by other evil powers. In some communities, adolescence is recognized by circumcision or by transitional roles assigned in acknowledgment of the move from childhood to adulthood. For example, the performance of such duties as herding or taking the family animals to the pastures is a task assigned during the transition stage for boys from childhood to adulthood.

Another important transition in one's life is from singleness to marriage. A Shona marriage is not just between two people, but it is the uniting of two families. One marries into a family. The birth of new

---

9 Murphree, *Christianity and the Shona*, 57.

10 Daneel, *Old and New in Southern Shona Independent Churches*, 154.

children in the family is seen as a sign of perpetuation of the patriarchal family name. Taboos are used to control whom one can marry. In this book, the use of the word taboo is as defined by Raddcliffe-Brown an anthropological scholar, who refers to a taboo as a "ritual avoidance" or "ritual prohibition,"

> A ritual prohibition is a rule of behavior which is associated with a belief that an infraction will result in an undesirable change in the ritual status of the person who fails to keep the rule. . .there is the idea that it involves the likelihood of some minor or major misfortune which will befall the person concerned.[11]

For example, it is a taboo for people of the same blood relations or same totem (animal, plant or object which is an emblem for a family) to marry. If marriage happens between related people, then a ritual *chekaukama* is performed to officially "cut" the original blood ties or the relationship.

There are no rituals marking transition into the position of "eldership" in a family. As one grows older, through leadership and life experiences, one is expected to gain wisdom with age and to attain the role of the "elder." Death is the final stage or transition from this physical life into the next world, the Spirit World. Burial, memorial, and cleansing rituals surround the death.

Other rituals not associated with the life cycle are related to the land. The rain ritual, *mukwerere* is performed if the rains are late for the purposes of appeasing the spirits and asking God to bring the rains on time or to save the dying crops. A pre-planting ritual is also performed in which people take the seeds to be planted to the chief and the medicine person(s) in the village, praying through the ancestors to bless the seeds. The prayers in this ritual ask for the rains to fall on time. In addition, the prayers announce to "Mother Earth" that people are about to cut wounds into her with plows, but that no harm is intended. Also associated with crops are harvest thanksgivings, in which the giving of one's first produce from the fields is observed. No one is allowed to eat the first crops until the ritual of thanksgiving has been performed. The cleansing (*Chenura*, mentioned

---

11 A. R. Radcliffe-Brown, "Taboo," in William A. Lessa and Evon Z. Vogt, eds., *Reader in Comparative Religion: An Anthroplogical Approach* (New York: Harper and Row, 1972), 73-74.

earlier) is performed for the deceased. In all rituals there is always the use of drums, shakers, and dancing. Rituals are important for the traditional Shonas as a person develops through life and for the maintenance of harmony between humans, creation, and the Spirit World.

The Impact of Western Christianity on the Shonas' Religious Identity. This section recapitulates the advent of Western Christianity and colonization in the Shona context, focusing on some of the changes Christianity and colonization wrought in the Shona peoples. Since post-colonial issues continue to affect the formation of Shona personal and religious identity, it is important to note the impact of Western Christianity on the culture.

Daneel notes that the first missionary to make contact with the Shona people was a Portuguese named Father Goncalo da Silveira in 1561. He was also the first Christian martyr to die among the Shonas and was killed the same year he arrived. The Dominicans tried to continue the work of da Silveira without success. Other missionaries, such as Robert Moffat, concentrated on working with the Ndebele, another Bantu group found in the western and southern part of Zimbabwe. Around 1855, David Livingstone also began working with the Ndebeles. A wave of different missionary societies arrived in the area around the time of colonization, during the 1890s.[12] The impact of Christianity and its influence have been felt strongly since the time of colonization.

As they spread Christianity in non-Western worlds, most missionaries believed that the indigenous people, including the Shona people, were paganistic, heathenistic, non-religious, and animistic. This belief by most missionaries was incorrect because non-Western contexts were not without religion or religious practices before the advent of Christianity. The Shonas had a traditional religion prior to the arrival of Christianity and colonization. When Christianity was brought to Africa, missionaries did not seem to recognize that they were also bringing their Western culture. Thus, the Christianity brought to the Shona context was a Christianity heavily influenced by Westernization. Both the colonizers and the missionaries

---

12 Ibid., 26, 186 & 187.

believed that Africans, which included the Shonas, were less human than missionaries. Besides being heathen, the Shonas were believed also to be savages, cannibalistic, animal-like in their behavior, and barbaric. The colonizers and missionaries believed the best thing they could do for such a people was to tame the "animal in the African." One way to accomplish this was to introduce Western civilization; i.e., to provide an educational system that would train the Shona to think as Europeans, learning European history, culture, and literature (such as Shakespeare), and Christianity.

As Whidborne, who has written on religion in Southern Africa, says about the missionary approach: "The European missionaries came to Africa to convert the heathen to Christianity, an attempt at replacing the traditional religion and culture in its entirety by Western Christianity."[13] One of the ways to "humanize" the Shonas was to teach the Shonas "good" religion, Christianity, and to have the Shonas literally abandon their "paganistic" surroundings (the village) and traditional religious practices. Zvobgo, a Shona, who writes about the common missionary attitude and beliefs, says:

> . . .missionaries did not understand, and did not bother to understand at the beginning, the African society which they came to evangelize. . .[they] assumed that Africans either had no religion at all, or that they had only a vague conception of the existence of a Supreme Being.[14]

Zvobgo further quotes one of the missionaries, Shimmin, who wrote that: ". . .these people with centuries of barbarism behind them, and with the bias of their moral nature so set against godliness are at first incapable of comprehending even those plain religious facts which appear so self evident to every Christian child."[15]

With missionaries using this type of approach, Christianity subverted healthy aspects of communal interpersonal relations basic to the center of

---

13 Vicki Whidborne, "Africanization of Christianity in Zimbabwe," *Religion in Southern Africa* 4 (Jan 1993): 31 & 64.

14 C. J. M. Zvobgo, "The Influence of the Wesleyan Methodist Missions in Southern Rhodesia, 1891-1923," in J. A. Dachs, ed., *Christianity South of the Zambezi*, vol. 1 (Gweru: Mambo Press, 1973), 64.

15 Ibid., 65.

Shona existence, both religiously and culturally. Illustrative of this subversiveness was a change in the understanding of salvation. The Shona traditional understanding of salvation considered it a communal event while Christianity's emphasis was on salvation as an individualistic personal concept. Murphree, a Methodist missionary and former professor at the University of Zimbabwe, notes the changes this notion of salvation had on the indigenous Shona:

> Conversion to Christianity was usually individual, and at conversion the individual frequently moved out of his tribal milieu into the society of the mission station. . .The Methodist emphasis on a subjective personal experience of conversion meant that the church did not attempt mass conversions or baptisms, rather. . .an attempt was made to lay the Methodist Gospel before the Budjga [a subgroup of the Shona] in such a way that they would accept it individually.[16]

Contrary to traditional beliefs, that an individual's salvation meant the family's salvation, individuals could now be saved while their whole family might be condemned by the wrath of God. Bhila, a Ndebele writer from Zimbabwe, arrives at the following conclusion about the activities of missionaries:

> The early missionaries paid scant attention to the complex, and often highly organized, systems of the religious cults among the African peoples. They erroneously believed that Africans "had no concepts of religion," and ascribed their slow progress in converting Africans to Christianity to what they called the "depraved habits" and the low intelligence of Africans.[17]

The problem created by the approach of the missionaries was that it placed the Shona between two conflicting religions and world-views. On the other hand, the Shonas may have liked the new Christian religion and wanted to convert to it, but conversion meant abandoning that which was familiar and was known, since the Shona traditional beliefs and culture were condemned by Christianity.

---

16 Murphree, *Christianity and the Shona*, 9.

17 Hoyini Bhila, "Trade and the Early Missionaries in Southern Zambezi," in M. F. C. Bourdilion, ed., *Christianity South of the Zambezi*, vol. 2 (Gweru: Mambo Press, 1977), 39.

Several different reactions of the Shonas to Christianity were apparent: rejection of Christianity and its values; acceptance of Christianity; ambivalence towards it; or acceptance with modifications (African Independent churches). For example, most of the United Methodists who converted to Christianity fell in the category of acceptance since this was the norm set by the missionaries. The current impact of missionary Christianity on the Shona can be seen in the United Methodist members who today find themselves caught between Christianity and African Traditional Religion. For example, in *The Central Africa Book of Discipline*, the following are to be adhered to: no smoking, no drinking alcohol, and no polygamy.[18] It is common knowledge that a Shona United Methodist Christian is not allowed to participate in *zvinhu zwechivanhu* (traditional Shona religious cultural activities), such as pouring of libation, rituals of *chenura* (cleansing ritual), or honoring of or praying through ancestors. The prohibition of church members participating in such activities results from the condemnation of the traditional rituals and religio-cultural activities still considered paganistic by the Shona Christian church today.

Chavhunduka, a Shona sociologist and former Vice-Chancellor of the University of Zimbabwe who believes in traditional medicine, in addressing the impact of Christianity and Western education on the Shona Christians, notes that,"...many people are now ashamed of revealing their connections with traditional practitioners because of the stigma attached to traditional treatment." Chavhunduka relates a story of a sick individual, who claimed to be a Christian, who vowed she would not consult traditional practitioners or medicine people because only "heathens" would do that. A few days later, Chavunduka met the woman at a medicine person's home. When he confronted her about her Christianity, she responded by saying there was nothing wrong with just consulting.[19]

---

18 Ronald P. Patterson ed., *The Book of Discipline of the United Methodist Church: Africa Central Conference Edition* (Nashville: The United Methodist Publishing House), 1990, 44 & 53.

19 G. L. Chavhunduka, "Traditional Medicine and Christian Beliefs," in M.F.C. Bourdilion, ed., *Christianity South of the Zambezi*, vol 2 (Gweru: Mambo Press 1977), 134 -136.

Chavhunduka contends that there is an awareness among Shona Christians that certain medicines of traditional practitioners are effective. Nevertheless, the church says Christians cannot use or consult traditional practitioners for such. The Shona Christians, when faced with situations such as life or death, find themselves in a psychological dilemma about whether to comply with Western Christian guidelines or to engage in Shona Traditional methods.

Chavhunduka gives other examples, from his personal experiences, of people who were strong Christians, and some who were leaders in the church, whom he observed in a struggle between their Western Christian values and their Shona traditional beliefs. He quotes a married couple who were leaders in a church, whom he saw consulting the traditional practitioners. After he confronted them, they responded:

> At least we are doing it publicly. There are many people in the church, including some ministers, who consult these traditional practitioners at night and condemn them in their church sermons. We know some prominent members of the church-'educated people'-who have been to the *n'anga* but do not want people to know about it.[20]

Even though the Christian church is led by the Shona people, the approach and doctrines have not changed much from what was established by the Western missionaries. The readily noticeable changes include the incorporation of some worship songs composed by the indigenous people, the use of drums and shakers (*ngoma nehosho)* respectively, originally prohibited), clapping of hands, and dancing during worship. However, some of the convictions by missionaries, regarding the traditional African religious beliefs and values as heathen, are maintained by the Shona Christian church today. This situation perpetually casts the urban Shona Christians into a dilemma about healing in times of crisis.

The above missionary approach was also used in the educational system with the backing of the church. The missionaries believed that the most effective approach to convert the Shonas was to change both their religious values and psychological awareness of themselves. Father

---

20 Ibid., 137.

Shropshire, who wrote extensively on missionary activities in the early part of the 1900s in Southern Africa (including Zimbabwe), says:

> Not until a truly Christian and scientific education has corrected the balance of the present Native psychological complex, and enabled the Africans to meet their phobias with a critical mind, giving them confidence in themselves and ability to control their own environment, will they come to see that the wonders of magic and sorcery are not so marvelous as wonders of a truly and proportionately developed personality, the more especially if that personality at the same time maintains the true 'abundant' of the fullest Christian life.[21]

Both missionaries and colonizers, as per Father Shropshire's statement, truly believed Bantus (which included the Shonas) were very primitive and were inferior to Europeans. The agenda of the missionaries was to reach and change the mind-set of the children while still young in order for effective conversion to take root. At the same time, the educational goals of the colonizers were not as beneficial for the African peoples. Instead, education contributed to bringing Shona people down to a level where they could be "used" by the colonizer as a tool, and still be reminded that they (the Africans) were inferior to the Europeans, despite the Africans' achievements in the process.

This psychological and spiritual dilemma, in part, is what this book is attempting to address. How does the pastoral caregiver help people in such a religious crisis? The Shona Christian may believe in the possibility of the medicine person's ability to cure their illness, or might have witnessed others being cured of an illness after having consulted traditional practitioners. When equipped with an integrative consciousness, pastoral caregivers address these conflictual issues, both personally and communally, for those in crisis, and can challenge the church to re-examine its doctrines and stance.

The Impact of Colonialism on Shonas' Personal Identity. In this section this writer will make reference to some of the discourse taking place in present Africa, particularly in relationship to the crisis of post-colonial

---

21 W. T. Shropshire, *The Church and the Primitive Peoples* (London: Macmillian, 1938), 421-22.

identity. My stand is that colonialism had an impact on the current situation in most of Africa, including the present Zimbabwe. Much debate continues on the question of what post-colonialism means, but the focus here is not on the debate about whether there is anything called post-colonial discourse or neo-colonialism.

Scholars debate about the use of the term "post-colonialism" and this author agrees with the way Shohat defines this term:

> . . .the "post-colonial" implies both going beyond anti-colonial nationalist theory as well as a movement beyond a specific point in history, that of colonialism and Third World nationalist struggles. In that sense the prefix "post" aligns the "post-colonial" with another genre of "post"-post-war, "post-cold war". . .all of which underline a passage into a new period and a closure of certain historical event or age, officially stamped with dates.[22]

It is up to the reader to categorize this period as post-colonial or neo-colonial. I am more interested in the effects and/or impact of colonialism on Zimbabwe before and after independence. Educational social systems and cultural changes in independent Zimbabwe, caused by the effects of colonialism, are still felt today. These changes are the primary concerns of this writer.

Mungazi, a Shona historian and educator, traces the coming of colonialism to Africa in general, and to Zimbabwe in particular. He suggests that the mind-set of the colonizers or Europeans about Africans can be captured this way:

> They equated the universal man with themselves; Europeans were synonymous with the universal man. Although emphasis on the study of man formed a philosophy known as humanism, the concept of humanity excluded the African until studies were conducted to determine whether they were actually human.[23]

---

22 Ella Shohat, "Notes on the Post-Colonial," *Social Text* 31/32 (1992): 101. For further discussion on the debate about post-colonialism or neo-colonialism see also P. Williams and L. Chrisman, eds., *Colonial Discourse and Post-colonial Theory: A Reader* (New York: Columbia University Press, 1994).

23 Dickson Mungazi, *The Mind of Black Africa* (London: Praeger, 1997), 27.

Mungazi goes on to elaborate about the mind-set and beliefs of the pioneers of colonization in Zimbabwe from 1890 to the period of independence 1980.[24] He quotes Rhodes, who got a standing ovation in 1896 for saying in a parliamentary debate in Capetown:

> "I say that the Natives are like children. They are just emerging from barbarism. They have a human mind, but they are like children, and we ought to do something to develop that mind. . .We have to treat the Natives where they are, in a state of barbarism. We are to be lords over them. We will continue to treat them as subject race as long as they continue to be in a state of barbarism."[25]

Even in these modern days there are those who continue to reinforce such racist mentalities by publishing studies claiming that all peoples of African descent are inferior to the White race. A case in point is the publication of authors Herrnstein and Murray who claim that Black people are of inferior intelligence to the Whites.[26] The proclaimed mind set about Africans by Rhodes gave power to all the Europeans residing in then Rhodesia, including to a lot of the missionaries. In this way, Rhodes provided the Westerners with grounds to treat Africans unjustly.

Similarly Huggins, who was prime minister of colonial Zimbabwe in the 1930s to the early 1950s, is quoted as saying:

> "We must unhesitatingly accept the doctrine that our superiority over the Natives rests on the color of our skin, civilization and heredity. We must appreciate that we have a paramount monopoly of these qualities and that the natives have been denied them by their primitive culture. You can call me an imperialist of the old school. True imperialism entails paternal government. It would be outrageous to give the Native a so called political partnership when he is likely to ruin himself as a result."[27]

---

24 Ibid., 27, Mungazi discusses the mentality of Rhodes, Huggins and finally Smith, who were Prime Ministers of Rhodesia at different time periods.

25 Ibid.

26 Richard J.Herrnstein and Charles Murray, *The Bell Curve: Intelligence and Class Structure in American life* (New York: Free Press, 1994).

27 Mungazi, *The Mind of Black Africa*, 29.

Huggins delivered the above statement as late as 1952. This cultural chauvinistic mentality would continue beyond Huggins' era. Neither did it die with Smith's declaring independence from Britain (Unilateral Declaration of Independence) in 1964, nor Smith's appointment as Prime minister of Rhodesia until 1979. Smith's government deported bishops such as Ralph Dodge (United Methodist) who were arguing for the rights of the Africans in then Rhodesia. The Prime Minister's argument was that he did not believe that the Africans possessed an intellect and culture similar and equal to that of the Europeans.[28]

Much of this mentality and belief in the superiority of the "White man, his culture and language,"is still pervasive in Zimbabwe today, even among some of the Shona people, as indicated by earlier quotations from the newspapers in 1996. This mindset is one from which a lot of the younger generation, growing up in the urban Shona context, need to be decolonized. Decolonization means freeing people from the mental oppression of believing in the superiority of the colonizer (the Western people) and the inferiority of the indigenous people in every sense or form.

One of the most noticeable signs of what this author sees as cultural colonialism in the present Zimbabwe is the use of the English language. In schools as well as in homes, children are taught to learn English rather than their mother language. Ngugi wa Thiongo, an author of African Literature from Kenya (a former British colony), correctly argues that one of the tools used by the colonizer to complete colonization was forcing European languages on the colonized. wa Thiongo states that the colonized thought, and still think, that the more articulate one becomes in speaking these colonial languages, the more intelligent one is. He also discusses how African traditional languages were used in traditional African societies to educate children, and how this has changed with the coming of the Western educational system. wa Thiongo wrote:

> Language was not a mere string of words [in traditional society]. It had a suggestive power well beyond the immediate and lexical meaning. . .The language through images and symbols, gave us a view of the world. . .And then I went to school, a colonial school, and this harmony was broken. The language of my education was no longer the language of my culture. . .English became more than

28 Ibid., 19.

> a language: it was the language, and all the others had to bow before it in deference.[29]

Thus, English became the medium for instruction in schools, even for the teaching of native languages. In Zimbabwe, for example, the Shona language is taught using English. One of the most fundamental implications for the use of English, again, as wa Thiongo observes, is that it produces self-alienation of African children, alienating them from their language of familiarity through the use of English:

> It starts with. . .dissociation of the language of conceptualisation. . .of mental development, from language of daily interaction in the home and the community. It is like separating mind from the body so that they are occupying two unrelated linguistic spheres in the same person. . .it is like producing a society of bodiless heads and headless bodies.[30]

Thus, colonization, as per wa Thiongo's statement, produces divided cultural and personal identities in the African. I concur with wa Thiongo and believe that language influences one's understanding of a culture, one's epistemology, and that it is the medium through which culture and epistemology are communicated. Because the instruction of the children is in English, the Western educational system exacerbates identity conflict for children who are not fully cognizant of their Shona language, culture, and history.

Memmi, a Tunisian Jew who wrote about anti-colonialism and the impact of colonialism on both the colonizer and the colonized, airs similar sentiments about the implications of the type of colonial education for the colonized. He notes:

> The memory which is assigned him is certainly not of his people. The history which is taught him is not his own. He knows who Colbert or Cromwell was, but he learns nothing about Khazanadar [local hero]. . .Everything seems to have

---

29 Ngugi wa Thiongo, *Decolonizing the Mind: The Politics of Language in African* (Harare: Zimbabwe Publishing House, 1994), 11.

30 Ibid., 28.

> taken place out of his country. . .The books talk to him of a world which in no way reminds him of his own. . .[31]

Memmi also makes an insightful observation on the use of a second language in the education system of the colonized, and the mental or psychological effects of the second language on the same. He asserts that:

> Possession of two languages is not merely a matter of having two tools, but actually means participation in two psychical and cultural realms. Here, the two worlds symbolized and conveyed by the two tongues are in conflict; they are those of the colonizer and the colonized.
>
> Furthermore, the colonized's mother tongue, that which is sustained by his feelings, emotions and dreams, that in which his tenderness and wonder are expressed, thus that which holds the greatest emotional impact, is precisely the one which is least valued. It has no stature in the country or in the concert of peoples. If he wants to obtain a job. . .exist in the community and the world, he must first bow to the language of his masters. In the linguistic conflict within the colonized, his mother tongue is that which is crushed. He himself sets about discarding this infirm language, hiding it from the sight of strangers.[32]

This above statement by Memmi appears to be a prophecy fulfilled in the Shona context as per newspaper articles from 1996 quoted earlier. Among the urban Shonas, the impact of colonization is evidenced by the use of English language in schools, businesses, and generally by the majority of the younger generation. Colonization has stripped the younger generation of the pride of using or knowing their mother tongue. Memmi further addresses the devastating psychological effects of colonization on the personal or self-identity of the colonized:

> The first attempt of the colonized is to change his condition by changing his skin. . . .The first ambition of the colonized is to become equal to that splendid model and to resemble him [colonizer] to the point of disappearing in him. . .Rejection of self and love of another are common to candidates for assimilation. Moreover, the two components of this attempt at liberation are closely tied. Love of the colonizer is subtended by a complex of feelings ranging from shame to self-hate.[33]

---

31 Albert Memmi, *The Colonizer and the Colonized* (Boston: Beacon Press, 1991), 105.

32 Ibid., 107.

33 Ibid., 120-121.

Memmi is saying that the colonized internalize the idea that to be fully human, they have to lose cultural identity and take the identity of the colonizer. The colonized have to literally change, not just the skin color, but their mental or psychological functioning as well. He contends that colonization spiritually destroys, distorts, and kills even the colonized. Memmi observes:

> We have seen that colonization materially kills the colonized. It must be added that it kills him spiritually. Colonization distorts relationships, destroys or petrifies institutions, and corrupts men, both colonizer and colonized. To live the colonized needs to do away with colonization. To become a man, he must do away with the colonized being he has become. . .He must conquer himself and be free in relation to the religion of his group which he can retain or reject, but he must stop existing only through it. Finally, he must cease defining himself through the categories of colonizers.[34]

Many other writers on post-colonial discourse, such as Frantz Fanon, Aime Cesaire, and Ashis Nandi, have also written about the effects of colonialism on the colonized. Despite the different ways in which they approach this subject, they all seem to agree that people in former colonial countries need to move away from their colonial, oppressed, colonized minds to be whole again.[35]

In his writings, Fanon, a Martinique-born, black psychiatrist, social scientist and anti-colonialist has as his, main concern and focus the psychological destruction of the identity and consciousness of the colonized people by colonialism and its systems. He argues that physical domination in the colonized countries is self-evident. However, the more dangerous and pervasive domination, Fanon points out, is the psychological and mental domination. He states that physical domination can be removed by a revolution or other means, but mental and psychological oppression is too complex to remove because it is ingrained in the psyche and conscience of

---

34 Ibid., 151-152.

35 Ashis Nandi, *The Intimate Enemy: Loss and Recovery of Self under Colonialism* (Oxford: Oxford University press, 1983), see also Albert Memmi, *Colonizer and the Colonized* Boston: Beacon Press, 1991), Frantz Fanon, *The Wretched of the Earth* (New York: Grove Press, 1963), Aimc Cesaire, *Discourse on Colonialism* (English edition) (New York and London: Monthly Review Press, 1972).

the colonized. Even if the colonizer was to leave, mental colonization remains in place because it outlives the physical presence of the colonizer.[36] Fanon aptly observes that colonialism creates an "inferiority complex" in the natives which results in "the so called dependency complex of the colonized people." He argues however, that the colonized were not born with this complex; this is something that came as a result of the colonial system.[37] Fanon also notes the detrimental effects of colonization:

> Perhaps we have not sufficiently demonstrated that colonialism is not simply content to impose its rule upon the present and the future of a dominated country. Colonialism is not satisfied merely with hiding a people in its grip and emptying the native's brain of all form and content. By a kind of perverted logic, it turns to the past of the oppressed people, and distorts, disfigures and destroys it. This work of devaluing pre-colonial history takes on dialectical significance today. . .The effect consciously sought by colonialism was to drive into the natives' heads the idea that if the settlers were to leave, they would at once fall back into barbarism, degradation and beastiality.[38]

For Fanon, colonialism creates an empty shell mentally in the colonized. What then is replaced in this shell is the colonized's belief in the superiority of the colonizer. Part of this belief is that, if the colonizer was to leave, the colonized would not be able to function on their own. The basis for the identity of the colonized is the colonizer's history, culture, language, and religion. Colonialism creates self-alienation and identity dissonance as well as confusion about the self.

Fanon goes on to describe what the process of overcoming a colonial mentality might be. He says that the natives, especially the educated, start by trying to assimilate or emulate the European. This assimilation is even reflected by the type of writings they produce. In the process of emulating the Westerner, the indigenous people lose a lot of their cultural values but

---

36 Frantz Fanon, *The Wretched of the Earth* (New York: Grove Press, 1963), 210ff.

37 Frantz Fanon, *Black Skin White Masks* (New York: Grove Press, 1967), 83ff.

38 Frantz Fanon, "On National Culture," in P. Williams, & L. Chrisman, ed., *Colonial Discourse and Post-colonial Theory: A Reader* (New York: Columbia University Press, 1994), 37.

are not consciously aware that this is taking place. This initial stage described above he calls "unqualified assimilation."

When a native is disturbed by the unfulfilling processes of assimilation, s/he then tries to remember who s/he is and this marks the emergence of Fanon's stage two.

> This period of creative work approximately corresponds to that immersion which we have just described. But since the native is not a part of his people, since he only has exterior relations with his people, he is content to recall their life only. Past happenings of the bygone days of his childhood will be brought up out of the depth of his memory. . .but often too it is symptomatic of a period of distress and difficulty, where death is experienced and disgust too. We spew ourselves up. . .[39]

What Fanon addresses is similar to what is called in this book, a person's experience of the hybridity in the form of naive consciousness. A crisis results in someone being disturbed, disgusted, and distressed ultimately eventuating in a search for identity. The third and final stage of overcoming colonization is what Fanon calls "the fighting stage."

> . . .the native, after having tried to lose himself in the people and with the people, will in contrary shake the people. Instead of according the people's lethargy an honoured place in his esteem, he turns himself into an awakener of the people, hence comes a fighting literature, revolutionary literature and a national literature.[40]

This third stage is what this writer hopes a pastoral caregiver with an integrated consciousness possesses. The goal is for this individual to be fully aware of who s/he is, to be aware of the two cultures to which s/he has been exposed, and to use this integrative (critical) consciousness to help awaken and challenge the status quo.

Cesaire, the best known poet in the French Caribbean, and a writer as well as an elected politician, says the following about evils of colonialism:

> Between colonizer and colonized there is room only for forced labor, intimidation, pressure, the police, taxation, theft, rape, compulsory crops, contempt, mistrust,

39 Fanon, "On National Culture," 41.

40 Ibid., 41.

> arrogance, self-complacency, swinishness, brainless elites, degraded masses. No human contact, but relations of domination and submission which turn the colonizing man into a classroom monitor. . .slave driver, and the indigenous man into an instrument of production.
>
> My turn to state an equation: colonization = "thing-ification.". . .I am talking about societies drained of essence, cultures trampled underfoot, institutions undermined, lands confiscated, religions smashed and magnificent artistic creations destroyed, extraordinary possibilities wiped out.[41]

Cesaire also makes a similar argument to Fanon's, that the Europeans or the colonizers believed and were convinced that the colonized people were born psychologically inferior to the colonizers. In an interview, Cesaire says that European writers such as M. Mannoni (Cesaire does not give title of the book he is discussing) believe in the dependency complex of the colonized and that Mannoni's negative notion needs to be argued against. Cesaire says:

> Follow him [Mannoni] step by step through the ins and outs of his little conjuring tricks, and he will prove to you as clear as day that colonization is based on psychology, that there are in this world groups of men who, for unknown reasons, suffer from what must be called dependency complex, that these groups are pyschologically made for depedence; that they need dependence, that they crave it, ask for it, demand it, that this is the case with most of the colonized peoples. . . .These Negroes can't even imagine what freedom is. They don't want it, they don't demand it. It's the white agitators who put that into their heads. And if you gave it to them, they won't know what to do with it.[42]

The above beliefs were not held by colonizer only, but also taught to the colonized; in the post-colonial context today these beliefs did not vanish with the coming of independence. Thus, the need for a search for identity in the post-colonial context is a result of the above theories of the inferiority of the colonized being ingrained and lodged in the psyche of the colonized. For Cesaire, the way to recover a cultural identity lost as a result of colonization in the post-colonial context is to reclaim the past history, culture elements, and values:

---

41 Cesaire, *Discourse on Colonialism*, 21.

42 Ibid., 39-41.

> We live in an atmosphere of rejection, [colonized and black people] and we developed an inferiority complex. I have always thought that the black man was searching for his identity. And it has seemed to me that if what we want is to establish this identity, then we must have a concrete consciousness of what we are-that is, of the first fact of our lives: that we are black; that we were black and have a history, history that contains certain cultural elements of great value. . .in sum, we assert that our Negro heritage was worthy of respect, and that this heritage was not relegated to the past, that its values were values that could still make an important contribution to the world. . .R.D. [Rene Depestre]: Certainly, because the relationships between consciousness and reality are extremely complex. That's why it is equally necessary to decolonize our minds, our inner life, at the same time that we decolonize society.[43]

It is fair to conclude that, because of the impact of colonialism on some of the urban contemporary Shona people, they suffer from an inferiority complex, believing that the Western way of life is the right one and the Shona traditional way has to be relegated into the past.

Writing from the context of India, another former British colony, Nandi, a psychoanalyst, gives an example of the problem of colonization by writing about a man he calls Kipling, who is caught between cultures. In this illustration he addresses the psychological and mental impact of colonization on the colonized. He says:

> Kipling's dilemma can be stated simply: he could not be both Western and Indian; he could be either Western or Indian. It was this imposed choice which linked his self-destructiveness to the tragedy of his life: Kipling's avowed values were Western, his rejected under-socialized self Indian, and he had to choose between the two. Had it been the other way round he might have managed as a brown sahib or as a babu at least to acknowledge his bi-cultural self and reconcile however crudely the East and the West within him.[44]

Kipling is a photographic parallel to what I see as happening in the urban contemporary Shona context. Some of the Shonas in the urban context are "under-socialized" when it comes to the Shona traditional culture. Consequently, they cannot claim to be traditional Shonas nor can they claim to be Western. Nandi suggests that people such as Kipling are caught in a psychological battle of having no identity based on culture and/or

---

43 Ibid., 76 & 78.

44 Nandi, *The Intimate Enemy*, 71.

religion. Urbanization, in fact, compounded the situation where the Shona lost their culture.

Colonization also brought urbanization. The Westernized cities did not match the village life, thereby changing the social structures and systems of the people. In place of extended families in the villages, nuclear and individualistic family systems became prominent in the cities. This urban context runs contrary to the Shona way of life where communal existence in the village settings is central to one's sense of being or wholeness. Contemporary urban Shonas find themselves existing in a *bi-cultural* and *bi-religious* context: they live in the tension of traditional Shona and Western cultures, as well as that of Shona traditional religion and Western Christianity.

Colonization and colonial mentality were and are detrimental to one's identity, for they strip one of personal or religious identity. The best way to be rid of this mental oppression is to be decolonized of such a mind-set as suggested by Fanon above. My hope is that an integrated consciousness is one which is also decolonized, as well as free of mental oppression by the colonial ideological thinking that everything Western is superior to the traditional Shona religio-culture.

Crisis hits when the Shona people start to search for their personal identity. Having been raised in a hybrid culture (in the form of naive consciousness), with the European culture considered superior, such people are caught in an identity crisis. It is the hope of this writer that a pastor who is trained and possesses an integrative consciousness (critical consciousness) will help the parishioner in resolving this identity crisis, since the pastor is trained in the awareness of or identification of the struggles involved.

In conclusion, in this chapter I have presented a synopsis of the Shona traditional religio-culture, a brief historical presentation of the coming of colonization and Western Christianity, and an introductory discussion of the impact of Western Christianity and colonization on the contemporary urban Shona context. My argument is not that the Shonas' religion and culture were eradicated by the coming of colonization and Christianity, but rather that they were fundamentally changed in the urban Shona context, thereby creating a hybrid Christianity and culture for the urban Shonas, to be addressed by new pastoral care paradigms possessed by those with an integrative consciousness (critical consciousness).

The bi-cultural and bi-religious context in which the urban Shonas find themselves creates anxiety. As presented in Chapter One, anxiety sends the contemporary urban Shonas to the pastoral caregiver. My theory about anxiety and pastoral theology of care in the Shona context relates to Sullivan's theory of anxiety presented in detail in the next chapter:

> . . .it is anxiety which is responsible for a great part of the inadequate, inefficient, unduly rigid, or otherwise unfortunate performances of people; that anxiety is responsible in a basic sense for a great deal of what comes to a psychiatrist for attention. Only when this is understood, can one realize that this business of whether one is getting more anxious or less is in a large sense the basic influence which determines interpersonal relations. . .it more or less directs the course of their development.[45]

Anxiety produced by dysfunctional interpersonal relationships is apparent in the Shona urban context because of the effects of bi-culturalism and bi-religiousness. As a result, most contemporary Shona Christians arrive at their pastor's door seeking care for issues of personal and religious identity confusion. The next chapter addresses the issues of personal identity confusion and anxiety experienced by the urban contemporary Shonas.

---

45 Sullivan, *Interpersonal Theory of Psychiatry*, 160.

CHAPTER THREE

Interpersonal Relations and Personal Identity Development

Munhu vanhu, is a Shona saying which translates to "a person is because of other people." This saying illuminates the way Shona people define the self.[1] One's identity is defined out of one's community of "embeddedness."[2] Other common African sayings support the idea that the world-view, philosophy, and self-understanding of most Africans, including the Shonas, is community based: "I am because we are, and since we are, therefore I am;" "One tree does not make a forest;" "A charcoal or coal gets its burning energy from being in the fire of others." Out of interpersonal relations, one develops an individual identity. Humans get their vitality, their physical, social, psychological and spiritual security and their identity from being in healthy interpersonal relationships with others.

The primary focus of this chapter is to present Sullivan's theory of interpersonal relations and personal identity development, and to explore

---

1 Self in this book means how one sees oneself based on one's physical, mental, psychological, spiritual make-up and in one's relationship to the spirit world and all of creation.

2 Robert Kegan, *The Evolving Self: Problem and Process in Human Development* (Cambridge: Harvard University Press, 1982), 115-6. The phrase "community of embeddedness"is appropriated in this book in a similar sense as Kegan uses it in referring to a "culture of embeddedness." He defines this as a "psychosocial environment or the holding environment." He says that it is a particular form of the world or context in which or out of which a person grows and evolves psychologically and socially.

how his theory can inform the pastoral caregiver in the urban Shona context. Sullivan's theory of interpersonal relations and personal identity development defines individuals in the context of their community of embeddedness (as does the Shona traditional understanding). When one examines the concepts of person through the developmental phases presented by Sullivan's theory, as well as the Shona traditional culture, it is what the community does and the person's positive response to the community values, morals and norms which is understood to create a personal identity. From birth to death, the community is crucial in providing interpersonal relations which contribute to the formation of a person's identity. However, the roles an individual plays, and the values and mores of the community one internalizes, also mold one's formation of individual identity. In short, one's personality or personal identity is formed in the interaction of interpersonal relationships, the internalization of family and community values, and personal experiences within a community.

The importance of Sullivan's theory is not whether his developmental stages are identical in every respect to those of the traditional Shona. Instead, what is significant are the three concepts of his theory which address the issues of communal existence, anxiety, and interpersonal relations; they are the missing links, lost as a result of the infiltration of the Western cultural values within the contemporary urban Shona context. Sullivan's idea that frequent unhealthy communal interpersonal relationships produce unhealthy anxiety is one of his key propositions used in this book.

One of the reasons Sullivan's theory is more suitable than other Western theories for the Shona context is its broader definition of the individual. This makes his theory more compatible to the Shona context, more so than most of the Western psychodynamic theories which narrowly define an individual as a self-contained entity. Western psychodynamic theories such as Freud's and Allport's are very individualistic.[3] The main focus of these western theories is the self-contained individual.

Background Problem to Personal Identity in the Urban Shona Context

The introduction of alien and foreign western understandings of the self has resulted in identity confusion for the contemporary urban Shona. Due to their minds being infiltrated by colonization, modernization, and Westernization, some of the contemporary urban Shonas have lost some of the Shona traditional understandings of what it means to be a person. Chidyausiku, a Zimbabwean who has written books in both Shona and English, writes about the dangers of the fast changes taking place in contemporary Zimbabwe. As stated earlier, he is of the mind-set that the infiltration of the Western culture upon the Shona people is detrimental:

> We the Shona have a culture which is in danger of being forgotten. Nursed within a colonial context many of us have come to think that 'the nanny is better than the mother.' We are now going through a period of transformation which affects all aspects of our way of life as it was in the past and as it has persisted to this very day. . .It is very sad to witness how this heritage is now being eroded and in danger of getting lost. If we are not careful, our generation may become like a dying tree with *broken roots*.[4]

In this quote Chidyausiku refers to the effects of the Western culture and its erosion of the Shona culture, leaving people with broken roots from their culture of embeddedness. In Chidyausiku's metaphor of the mother and the nanny, the mother represents the traditional Shona culture and the nanny represents the Western culture. This book argues that the urban Shonas are at a crossroads for they do not have enough knowledge of either the "mother" or the "nanny."

---

3 Sigmund Freud, *An Outline of Psychoanalysis* (New York: W. W. Norton & Co. Inc. 1949), 13 -24, 103 -124; Gordon Allport, *Personality: A Psychological Interpretation* (New York: Henry Holt, 1937).

4 Paul Chidyausiku, *Broken Roots: A Biographical Narrative on the Culture of the Shona People in Zimbabwe* (Gweru: Mambo Press, 1984), vii & viii.

One of the reasons for identity confusion is found in the fact that the starting points of self definition for personal identity in the two cultures (traditional Shona and Western) are different. The term "identity confusion" for this book means that a person is not sure who s/he is because that individual is caught between two conflicting social systems upon which their self definition is based. The Shonas define the self based on their community of embeddedness and the notion of "we." In the West, one's sense of self is centered in an understanding of the "I," with the emphasis on the individual.

There are Western theorists, such as M. Mead, E. Erikson, G. H. Mead, and H. S. Sullivan, whose views of being human or of self-definition are more communally-oriented than others.[5] I am arguing that such communally-oriented theories are the ones that can provide the Shona urban pastoral caregivers with suitable theories to use for this context.

I find Sullivan's theory in many respects compatible to the traditional Shona view of being human or personal self definition.[6] Sullivan's theory is used in this book to help inform and provide the Shona pastoral caregivers with a Western theory which can appropriately address issues arising from this transitional communally oriented Shona context. As a result of the pressures discussed earlier in this book (economics, conflict produced by the urban settings, the effects of hybridity, *bi-culturalism,* and *bi-religiousness)*, the contemporary urban Shona may choose not to tap into the traditional communal living wisdom and philosophy. Some contemporary urban Shonas would rather hang on to modernized scientific solutions, even in situations where they acknowledge that the traditional wisdom and philosophy may provide an answer. In addition, due to the lack of availability of written Shona literature, or communally oriented theories

5 George H. Mead, *Mind, Self and Society: From a Standpoint of Social Behaviorist* (Chicago: University of Chicago, 1962); see also E. Erikson, *Identity and the Life Cycle: Selected Papers* (New York: International Universities Press, 1959); Margaret Mead, *Growing up in New Guinea* (New York: A Mentor Book, New American Library, 1953); Harry S. Sullivan, *Interpersonal Theory of Psychiatry* (New York: W. W. Norton & Co. Inc., 1953).

6 Sullivan, *Interpersonal Theory of Psychiatry*, says, to be human is to in communal existence, 32 & 37.

which suit the Shona context today, some Shona pastoral caregivers try to apply individualistic theories borrowed from the West.

Most of the Western psychological theories influencing the field of pastoral theology of care and counseling have been criticized as being very individualistic. Pastoral theologians such as Larry Graham and others argue that Western theories in pastoral theology and care are individualistic and may not always fully address problems clients bring to the table, since the individualistic theories may miss the communal aspects of the presenting problem.[7] Bodian, a western psychotherapist, notes, "Some critics have also noted that the therapeutic world-view has surreptitiously suffused our cultural mainstream, helping to shift our values from a concern for community and communal good to an increasing preoccupation with individual fulfillment and personal growth."[8] In the same journal, Safransky, a Western psychotherapist, offers a similar critique:

> Therapy has become a kind of individualistic, self-improvement philosophy, a romantic ideology that suggests each person can become fuller, better, wiser, richer, and more effective. . .There are many who have located the roots of the therapeutic movement in the individualism embraced by the19th-century modernism, in which everyone is the author of his or her intentions and is responsible for his or her own life. Own. Own is a very big word in therapy; you own your life, as if there's a self, an individual, enclosed self, within a skin. That's individualism. That's the philosophy of therapy. I question that. The self could be redefined, given a social definition, a communal definition.[9]

Using the individualistic approach, criticized above, in the Shona context may not always work. These individualistic approaches or theories apply in very few instances, and in most cases they do not apply at all. This is because the contemporary urban Shona society is still very much caught

---

7 Illustrative of concerns in the field are: Pamela D. Couture and Rodney Hunter eds., *Pastoral Care and Social Conflict* (Nashville: Abingdon, 1995); Graham, *Care of Persons, Care of Worlds*, 1992.

8 Stephan Bodian, "Is Psychotherapy a Waste of Time," *The Yoga Journal* (May/June 1992): 50.

9 Sy Safransky, "Psychotherapy," *The Yoga Journal* (May/June 1992): 52 & 53.

between communal and individualistic social systems and world-views, leaving many of these people in a dilemma about which system to use.

In this fast changing society of the Shonas in Zimbabwe, a Shona pastoral caregiver with an integrated consciousness is cognizant of the fact that s/he can still tap into Shona traditional wisdom and philosophy. At times it is more appropriate for pastoral caregivers to use communally oriented approaches and blend them with individualistic ones. This is because, for example, the Shonas can be forced to *consciously* live individualistic lives due to urban pressures, while *subconsciously* (in their suppressed or repressed memory), they are aware that some of the communal living lifestyle is the ideal choice for them.

In short, the argument here is that being forced to live bi-cultural and bi-religious lives is creating religious and cultural dissonance for the Shonas. A definition of dissonance is that one finds himself or herself caught between two differing attractive opinions. When one is forced to choose that which is counter to one's belief system, dissonance occurs. Dissonance is based on the idea that individuals need consistency and balance in the function of their beliefs, knowledge, and attitudes. When new information is encountered which challenges the consistency of those beliefs and attitudes it results in dissonance:

> . . .dissonance results when an individual must select one of two equally attractive alternatives. . .dissonance arises when persons are forced to behave counter to their private [even public] attitudes. As a result, either the behavior or the attitude must change to bring cognitions into harmony.[10]

In the Shona context, dissonance is experienced religiously and culturally when one has to live with or choose between two contradictory, incompatible, or irreconcilable thoughts, or when one encounters inconsistency in one's beliefs or ideas. The conflict between Western religious culture and the Shona religio-culture creates dissonance at various levels for the Shona urban population. The resulting dissonance produces anxiety as one tries to deny the conflict to reconcile the differences in the

---

10 L. S. Brakensiek, "Cognitive Dissonance Theory," in Rodney J. Hunter, ed., *The Dictionary of Pastoral Care and Counseling* (Nashville: Abingdon Press, 1990), 188.

beliefs or ideas. For example, in the bi-cultural contemporary urban Shona context, conflict may be found in an attempt of self-definition. A Shona may find trouble defining himself or herself because their everyday way of life driven by economic pressures may be contrary to the sense of communal living found in the Shona traditional society.

Background to the Development of Sullivan's Theory

Sullivan drew not only from psychology, but from other fields of discourse. Recognizing the impact of these disciplines on his thought adds depth to understanding his theory. Sullivan is classified as a neo-Freudian. He was trained as a Freudian psychiatrist, but later modified Freud's theory saying it was inadequate in the understanding of human development and the treatment of pathology. Neo-Freudians compose a large group of analysts who adhered to the central principles of Freudian theory and premises, but expanded on and modified certain aspects of that theory.

Sullivan was also influenced by other theorists and by his personal experience as a practicing psychiatrist. As much as Sullivan was influenced by other theorists whose emphases were on the individual, one of his main contributions was to address the impact of communal interpersonal relations on the individual. Sullivan's theory of interpersonal relations, or his interpersonal approach in psychiatry, was influenced by the theories of Freud, Adolf Meyer, G. H. Mead, and Malinowski.

Sullivan notes that from Freud he gained the understanding of "the individual person as the central unit of study."[11] He also learned about instinctual drives and the libido, a theory he discarded later in the development of his own thought. Yet Sullivan was not enamored by the individual alone. Mullahy and Melinek studied and wrote on Sullivan's work and theories, and they note that ". . .it is not difficult to understand that the main unit of study for Freud is the more or less self-contained individual. For Sullivan, the unit of study is always an interpersonal

11 Sullivan, *Interpersonal Theory of Psychiatry*, 16.

situation or an ongoing series of interpersonal processes."[12] For Freud the center of study was the individual and his or her intrapsychic process.

These intrapsychic processes were mechanistic using physicalistic principles. In a "Project for Scientific Psychology," Freud's goal was to show that psychology is a natural science and that human minds operated like machines in the way they function or process. It would follow, according to Freud's theory of how the mind operates, that human behavior and personality are determined and mechanistic.[13] For Freud, there is always a cause to each human action, and human actions are always conscious or unconscious. Freud said early in his development of psychoanalytic ideas, "The intention is to furnish a psychology that shall be a natural science: that is, to present psychical processes as quantitatively determined states of specific material particles. . ."[14] As will be expounded later, for Sullivan it is not the self-contained individual's intrapsychic mechanistic functions that determine being a person; rather, it is the interpersonal relations that occur within interpersonal situations.

Sullivan also saw Freud's theory as closely connected to psychobiology. Psychobiology is the theory that there is a relationship between psychological and physical functioning of humans. Sullivan incorporated Adolf Meyer's theory of psychobiology into his theory of interpersonal relations. The following captures a few major points of Sullivan's understanding of Meyer's theory: "Psychobiology. . . Meyer is the study of man as the highest embodiment of mentally integrated life. . .Meyer stated specifically and succinctly that psychobiology is concerned with the individual human organism as a primary entity."[15] Sullivan agreed with the idea that to understand humans, one has to study the individual human organism. However, he believed this alone would not give us a full picture

---

12 P. Mullahy, and M. Melinek, *Interpersonal Psychiatry* (New York: SP Medical & Scientific Books, Spectrum Publications, Inc., 1983), 2.

13 Sigmund Freud, *The Standard Edition of the Complete Psychological Works of Sigmund Freud*, vol. 1 (London: The Hogarth Press, 1886-1899), 295.

14 Ibid.

15 Sullivan, *Interpersonal Theory of Psychiatry*, 16.

of what a human being is, unless this knowledge was gathered within a context of interpersonal relations and community.

Another theorist who influenced Sullivan was George H. Mead, a social psychologist whose theory emphasized the importance of social interactions. From Mead, Sullivan draws conclusions about how humans influence each other in becoming a self. Sullivan quotes Mead who says:

> "The capacity of the human organism to play the parts of others. . .is the basic condition of the genesis of the self. In playing the parts of others we react to our playing as well. When the organism comes to respond to its own role assumptions as it responds to others it has become a self. "[16]

In short, Mead suggests that we develop personal identities as a result of complex interactions with others. Our reactions toward other people's responses to our play and behavior, and how we in turn react to the roles we assume, play a great part in the formation of our individual identities. Individuals "internalize" the play, and from those behaviors they get positive responses from others who are within acceptable community norms and values.

From Malinowski, a cultural anthropologist, Sullivan draws upon the idea of human connection and the social rules and customs which tie human beings together:

> ". . .human beings are bound together by their connection with a definite portion of environment, by their association with a common shelter and by the fact that they carry out certain tasks in common. This concerted character of their behavior is a result of social rules, that is customs. . ."[17]

Malinoswki's cultural anthropological understanding aided Sullivan in comprehending and incorporating into his theory the influences of culture on human beings in the midst of personal identity development. Established social rules and customs assist in formulating characteristics of one's

---

16 Ibid., 17.

17 Ibid., 18, Sullivan cites, Bronislaw Malinowski, "Culture," in *Encyclopedia of Social Sciences*, (The Macmillan Company, 1930), 622.

actions, and in the process aid in the establishment of one's personal identity.

As stated earlier, Sullivan recognized how much he borrowed from other fields involved in the study of humans in developing his own theory. For Sullivan, all other theories lacked the interpretation of the impact of *interpersonal relations and situations* (elaborated later) in personal identity formation. Sullivan therefore concluded:

> Thus as psychobiology seeks to study the individual human being, and as cultural anthropology, which has been a powerful tributary to social science, seeks to study the social heritage shown in the concerted behavior of people making up a group, so psychiatry-and its convergent, social psychology-seeks to study the biologically and culturally conditioned. . .interpersonal processes occurring in the interpersonal situations in which the observant psychiatrist does his work.[18]

Thus, in addition to the study of the biological and cultural influences, Sullivan argues that one has to consider how interpersonal relationships influence personal identity formation.

Communal Existence, Anxiety and Interpersonal Relations in Personal Identity. Sullivan defines humans as *social beings* who cannot survive without *interpersonal relations*. He uses words such as *interactions* and *interchange* to define interpersonal relations and situations.[19] There is reciprocity or an interpersonal exchange taking place in an interpersonal situation. An interpersonal situation is the condition under which the relational exchange between persons occurs.

Sullivan gives an example of a mother feeding a baby as an interpersonal situation in which an interpersonal relationship is also taking place. There is more than feeding transpiring; there are also interactions or relational exchanges, bonding, or emotional, physical and psychological connections between the mother and the infant. Wherever there is interaction, reciprocity, or communication between humans, there is an interpersonal relationship taking place. However, the relationship may be

---

18 Ibid., 20.

19 Ibid., 32.

positive or negative. The negative relationships are the ones that result in anxiety. The development of anxiety becomes an important notion and will reappear in this book.

Directly connected to interpersonal relationships, Sullivan borrows from Freud the concept of instincts. Sullivan says that human beings, like other animals, are born with instincts. However, the instincts in humans are to be qualified by the word *human* because they are different from those of other animals. Sullivan calls these instincts *human instincts*. The human instincts are instincts to *relate*. The instincts to *relate* are different from Freud's *instinctual drives*. Freud notes about an instinct:

> An instinct differs from a stimulus in that it arises from sources of stimulation within the body, operates as a constant force, and is such that the subject cannot escape from it by flight as he can from an external stimulus. An instinct may be described as having a source and an aim. The source is a state of excitation within the body and its aim is to remove that excitation; in the course of its path from its source to the attainment of its aim the instinct becomes operative mentally. We picture it as a certain sum of energy forcing its way in a certain direction.[20]

The example Freud gives as a way to satisfy an instinctual stimulation is through activities such as eating, having sex, and drinking. However, Freud does not say that an instinctual drive can be permanently removed by satisfying it once, since "it arises from the sources of stimulation within the body," which are still present and can again be excited.

In his later writings, Freud also says there are two basic instincts, the life (Eros) instinct and the death (Thanatos) instinct. The life instinct is the "instinct of self-preservation and of the preservation of the species," examples being, hunger, sex, and thirst. The aim of the second instinct (death), "is to undo connections and so to destroy things," examples being, suicide, aggression, and hatred of others.[21] He further says,

---

20 Sigmund Freud, *New Introductory Lectures on Psychoanalysis* (New York: W. W. Norton & Company, Inc. Publishers, 1933), 132-133.

21 Sigmund Freud, *An Outline Of Psychoanalysis* (New York: W. W. Norton and Company Inc., 1949), 20ff.

> We may picture an initial state of things by supposing that the whole available energy of Eros, to which we shall hence-forward give the name *libido*, is present in the as yet undifferentiated ego-id and serves to neutralize the destructive impulses which are simultaneously present.[22]

As much as Sullivan is borrowing the concept of instincts from Freud, for Sullivan the origin of the instinctual drives is not the libido. The base of the human instinct to relate is the connection between the biological being and the human environment. Sullivan does not give a direct definition of an instinct. However, he describes an instinct through its functions. Thus for example, in Sullivan's understanding, one of the main functions of human instincts is to be in good interpersonal relationships, contrary to the example of Freud's instinctual drive, such as sex, which one satisfies by having sex or sometimes engaging in sexual aggression. Sullivan notes about human instincts:

> There is abundant evidence that the human animal is not able to look after himself for a long time after birth; and that the abilities that characterize him are matured serially over a term of no less than ten to twenty years. The human animal is utterly dependent at birth and, diminishingly but still greatly, dependent on the tender cooperation of the human environment. . .The idea of "human instincts" in anything like the proper rigid meaning of maturing patterns of behavior which are not labile is completely preposterous. Therefore, all discussions of 'human instincts' are apt to be very misleading and very much a block to correct thinking, unless the term *instinct*, modified by the adjective *human*, is so broadened in its meaning that there is no particular sense in using the term at all.[23]

Sullivan's use of the word instinct means general human tendencies which are inborn. Instincts are naturally inborn dispositions: acquired human tendencies are what make "human instincts" different from the Freudian use of the term "instinct." In other words, Sullivan is arguing that humans are interpersonal beings and cannot survive without interaction with others. The biological and psychological self interacts interpersonally with the social world. The importance of instincts to relate, as posed by Sullivan and for this book, as will be expounded, is that they play a major role in

22 Ibid., 22.

23 Sullivan, *Interpersonal Theory of Psychiatry*, 20-21.

personal identity development. From a developmental point of view Sullivan notes:

> . . .before speech is learned every human being, even those in the lower imbecile class, has learned certain gross patterns of relationship with parent, or with someone who mothers him [the infant]. Those gross patterns become the utterly buried but quite firm foundations on which a great deal more is superimposed or built.[24]

Sullivan notes that the relationship of the infant to the mothering one is very important since it is the "foundation" upon which one's personality is formed. The interactions between the mother and the baby make the two to connect emotionally and psychologically such that they can sense each other's increase in anxiety. The relationship between the mother and the infant is a basic example of how one could come to an understanding of, what we would term, Sullivan's interpersonal relations theory. There is reciprocity between the infant and the mothering one in the form of sensing anxiety.

The term anxiety is one Sullivan also borrows from Freud.[25] In discussing the sources and functions of anxiety, Freud notes the following:

> . . .anxiety arises directly out of the libido; that is to say, there is brought about that state of helplessness of the ego in the face of excessive tension arising from ungratified need which results, as in birth, in the development of anxiety, so that there is again a possibility, which although obvious is of no great consequence, that it is precisely the excess of unutilized libido that finds its discharge in the form of anxiety.[26]

For Sullivan, the source of anxiety is tension in interpersonal relationships. Where anxiety exists, for example, between the mother and the infant, it is defined as the tension in opposition to the relationship between the mother and the baby. The root cause of anxiety for Sullivan is tension in relationships between the individuals or between the mother and the baby.

---

24 Ibid., 6.

25 Sigmund Freud, *The Problem of Anxiety* (N.Y.: W. W. Norton & Co. Inc, 1936), 81.

26 Ibid.

Sullivan notes that, "...anxiety in the mother induces anxiety in the infant ...understand that the induced anxiety of the infant makes him more difficult and worrisome to care for, so that his behavior may seem to justify disparagement of the mother's work with him."[27] As it pertains to adults, anxiety is that tension which interferes with one's interpersonal relationships or threatens the *self-system.*

The *self-system* is a learned defense mechanism whose work is self-preservation. Borrowing from Freud, the functions of the *self-system* in Sullivan's theory are similar to the ego's defense mechanisms in Freud's theory. Freud notes:

> Just as the id is directed exclusively to obtaining pleasure, so the ego is governed by considerations of safety. The ego has set itself the task of self-preservation, which the id appears to neglect. It makes use of sensations of anxiety as a signal to give a warning of danger threatening its integrity...Thus the ego is fighting on two fronts: it has to defend its existence both against an external world that threatens it with annihilation and against an internal world that makes excessive demands.[28]

Similarly, the *self-system,* as defined by Sullivan, is a learned defense system in response to the mother or others; its aim is protecting the self psychologically, emotionally and mentally (in both children and adults). In other words, the self-system is an individual emotional and psychological defense structure or process. He says,

> The self-system thus is an organization of educative experience called into being by the necessity to avoid or to minimize (diminish) incidents of anxiety. The functional activity of the self-system. . .is primarily directed to avoiding and minimizing this disjunctive tension of anxiety, and thus indirectly to protecting the infant from this evil eventuality in connection with the pursuit of satisfaction.[29]

---

27 Sullivan, *The Interpersonal Theory of Psychiatry*, 114. Anxiety as defined by Sullivan means a "fear-like state,"which causes distress or discomfort by interference with one's interpersonal relationships. The disruption of an existence of good interpersonal relations results in tension, and the tension produces distress, the "fear-like state" anxiety, in the individuals involved. (9).

28 Freud, *An Outline of Psychoanalysis*, 110-112.

29 Sullivan, *The Interpersonal Theory of Psychiatry*, 165-166.

When one's security is threatened, anxiety triggers the self-system as a defense mechanism. He argues that when anxiety is constant, or when one is exposed to too much of it, then it becomes harmful, dangerous, or unhealthy. Sullivan claims that anxiety is one of the key disruptive forces in interpersonal relations. Too much anxiety or constant anxiety causes disequilibrium to the self.[30]

Since anxiety is experienced when one's sense of security is threatened, and since interpersonal relations are central to one's sense of security, anxiety arises when interpersonal relations are threatened. Sullivan says, "The point is that the self is approved by significant others, that any tendencies of the personality that are not so approved, that are in fact strongly disapproved, are dissociated from personal awareness."[31] What forces one to disconnect or disengage from choices that are disapproved by others is that these options interfere with one's interpersonal relations. In other words, Sullivan is saying the result of continued engagement in disapproved tendencies is anxiety. To avoid anxiety arising from situations that interfere with one's interpersonal relations, the inclinations are to disengage or separate from such situations, or disconnect them from personal awareness. Anxiety or anxiety-prone situations are present throughout life, and constant anxiety is the number one element which humans try to avoid.

Faulty interpersonal relations are a source of great anxiety because they interfere with or interrupt one's communal existence. Sullivan's theory of stages of personal identity development is connected to anxiety and communal existence. About communal existence Sullivan notes:

> The principle of communal existence refers to the fact that the living cannot live when separated from what may be described as their necessary environment. . .the fact is that the living maintain constant exchange through their bordering membranes with certain elements in the physicochemical universe around them; and the interruption of this exchange is tantamount to death of the organism. Thus

---

30 Ibid., 160.

31 Sullivan, *Conceptions of Modern Psychiatry*, 22.

> by the principle of communal existence I mean that all organisms live in continuous, communal existence with their necessary environment.[32]

Communal existence, as understood by Sullivan, does not relate to humans alone but to all that surrounds them. This author's understanding of the above statement by Sullivan is that all living things, including humans, depend upon each other for survival. Lack of exchange with other organisms (air, water, trees, soil etc.), Sullivan says, may cause death in human beings. We are interdependent upon our "universe" and "necessary environment." For human beings, the necessary environment is the human culture and that which surrounds them.

He also perceives communal existence as meaning those interpersonal relationships which exist between humans. Without communal existence or other humans, Sullivan says, the human personality would deteriorate:

> . . .it is possible to think of man as distinguished from plants and animals by the fact that human life - in a very real and not only a purely literary or imaginary sense - requires interchange with an environment which includes culture, . . .man is distinguished very conspicuously from other members of the biological universe by requiring interchange with a universe of culture, this means, in actual fact, since culture is an abstraction pertaining to people that man requires interpersonal relationships or interchange with others. . .It is a rare person who can cut himself off from mediate and immediate relation with others for long spaces of time without undergoing a deterioration in personality.[33]

In other words, Sullivan is suggesting that "no person is an island." To survive and to have an identity, humans need a culture and need to engage in interpersonal relationships. He further argues that:

> If one scrutinizes the performances of any child it will be evident that the child as a creature is existing in communal existence in or with an environment now importantly cultural in its composition. The cultural entities, so to speak, are part of the necessary environment. The human being requires the world of culture,

---

32 Sullivan, *The Interpersonal Theory of Psychiatry*, 31.

33 Ibid., 33.

> cannot live *and be human* except in communal existence with it. . . Other people are, therefore, an indispensable part of the environment of the human organism.[34]

Sullivan notes that even in adulthood the idea of the "individual" (to use his term) is an illusion. He notes,

> . . .the study of individual personality did not seem to be within the field of science, the only thing that seems amenable to scientific approach being the actions in interpersonal situations; that which someone does with me, that can be observed, both by me and by some objective third person - what goes on in that person, the unique peculiarity of his personality, seems to escape any method of science. . .[35]

Sullivan maintains his argument that the development of personality and identity must be closely connected to communal existence. He is saying that we cannot have an individual or the study of the meaning of an individual outside of his or her community of existence or interpersonal relations. For Sullivan it would be therefore a misconception to speak of an individual outside the community. Individuality can only be understood within the context of interpersonal relationships. How then are Sullivan's concepts of anxiety, interpersonal relations, and communal existence related to Sullivan's stages of personal identity development?

Interpersonal Relationships in Sullivan's Stages of Personality Development. The purpose of this section is to present the connection between interpersonal relationships, anxiety, and communal existence in some of Sullivan's stages of personal identity development. Beginning with conception and continuing through adulthood, it is how the mother, siblings, peers, and other adults interrelate and interact with an individual that helps the individual to develop a personal identity. In short, Sullivan is saying that communal existence, that is, the individual interaction and relations within his or her "community of embeddedness," formulates personal identity.

---

34 Sullivan, *Conceptions of Modern Psychiatry*, 18.

35 Ibid., 23.

Sullivan outlines seven stages of personality development before one reaches maturity. In these stages of development, Sullivan argues, interpersonal relationships play a central part. At each developmental stage the child, or adolescent, has to acquire healthy interpersonal relations in order to have a positive personal identity. Sullivan's developmental stages include infancy, childhood, the juvenile era, pre-adolescence, early adolescence, late adolescence, and adulthood or maturity. He does not elaborate on adulthood or the stage of maturity. Sullivan talks about the roles adults are expected to play in the other stages of human development (infancy through late adolescence).

Sullivan addresses how a child develops a sense of self based upon one's relationship with the mother in the developmental stage of infancy.[36] He talks about three aspects of a sense of a "*me*," "the good me," "the bad me," and "the not me," present from the time of infancy. He suggests:

> . . .these aspects of interpersonal cooperation require acculturation or socialization of the infant. Infants are customarily exposed to all of these [forms of anxiety-prone interpersonal situations] before the era of infancy is finished. From experience of these three sorts-with rewards, with the anxiety gradient, and with practically obliterative sudden severe anxiety-there comes initial personification of three phases of what presently will be me. . .Now, at this time, the beginning personifications of me are good-me, bad me and not me.[37]

According to Sullivan, the development of the *me* depends on the baby's sensing the anxiety in the mothering one. He says that even though it is complex or impossible to trace scientifically the anxiety from the baby to the mother, it is present. The "good mother," who has a good relationship with the infant, helps the infant *incorporate* in him/herself an image of the "good me." He also believes that children who grow up in nurturing environments with good interpersonal relations develop high self-esteem

36 Sullivan is writing in the 1950's when gender roles are clearly defined in terms of the mother taking care of the baby, unlike today where fathers can assume the role of the care taker. What is important here is not the question of who is caring for the baby, but the key is the context of the community or the nurturing one who provides healthy interpersonal relations.

37 Sullivan, *The Interpersonal Theory of Psychiatry*, 161.

and a good "self-system, which is the same as a good-me."[38] The low level of anxiety in the interpersonal relationship between the mother and the baby helps the infant develop a sense of a "good me."

He says that an interpersonal relationship between the two is important or the infant will be anxious and develop a negative personal identity or the "bad-me." Constant anxiety caused by the tension in relationship between the mother and the infant, or the absence of a relationship, has a negative impact on the personality of the infant. What Sullivan calls the "nasty mother" is the mother who constantly exposes the baby to tension relationships or situations. The baby reflects to the self the image of "bad me" from a "bad mother." Sullivan notes: "*Bad-me*, on the other hand, is the beginning personification which organizes experience in which increasing degrees of anxiety are associated with behavior involving the mothering one in its more-or-less clearly prehended interpersonal setting."[39] From poor interactions, one develops poor personal identity with a very low self-esteem.

In an environment where the mothering one is absent or is persistently and extremely anxious, the mother is perceived as the "evil mother." The relationship is so extremely anxious that the baby develops a sense of "not me." Sullivan notes:

> The rudimentary personification of not-me evolves very gradually, since it comes from the experience of intense anxiety-a very poor method of education. . .these experiences are largely truncated, so that what they are really about is not clearly known. Thus organizations of these experiences are marked by uncanny emotion-which means experiences which, when observed, have led to intense forbidding gestures on the part of the mother, and induced intense anxiety in the infant. . .[40]

Sullivan goes on to suggest that people exposed to this intense anxiety develop a "not me" and this type of *me* easily develops dissociative behavior. Pathology may develop as a result of the relationship between the

---

38 Ibid, 164.

39 Ibid., 162.

40 Ibid., 163.

mother and the infant combined with the level of anxiety to which the infant is constantly exposed.

The child makes the transition into childhood at two to five years of age, when one of the key factors becomes the development of language. Sullivan believes the little boy identifies with the male gender and the girls with the female, as prescribed by the society, at the same time. The child is now developing interpersonal relationships with others, other than the mother and the siblings. Sullivan says:

> During infancy, he [child] learns the grossest culture patterns about zonal and general needs. But throughout the era of childhood there is an increasing demand for his cooperation. The child is expected to do things which are brought to his attention or impressed on him as requirements for action by the authority-carrying environment-the mother, increasingly the father, and perhaps miscellaneous siblings, servants and what not.[41]

Childhood is a period in which the child is starting to be held accountable and responsible by those in authority. The authority figures are more than the mother and the father, and include the community at large. To use Sullivan's words, these are the "siblings, servants and what not." By the phrase "what not" I assume that Sullivan is referring to other persons in the community who may impress communal values, rules, and norms upon the child.

The juvenile stage, five to eight years, is school age. This is the stage in which the child learns about social relations and the respect of social norms, values, and rules, what ostracism means, co-operation, competition, and group feelings.[42] The child internalizes these values and rules in the further development of a sense of self. In addition, the child understands ostracism as brought upon him or herself if s/he chooses to be indifferent to the societal and community norms and values.

---

41 Ibid., 203. By zonal needs Sullivan is referring to physiological needs mostly realized through the senses, such as the need to be touched, eating (sucking on the mother's breast) etc., and to put it in Sullivan's words this is "organization of special sense apparatus, such as sight, special tactile sensitivities, gustatory or taste sensitivities, olfactory or smell sensitivities." (63).

42 Ibid., 227ff.

The next stage, pre-adolescence, from eight to eleven years, is marked by the need for intimate interpersonal relationships. One of the persons important at this stage is the "chum."[43] This is a person who is of the child's same sex but older, and who acts as a role model with whom the child can confide and identify. Peer relationships are also important for the child. According to Sullivan, pre-adolescence and early adolescence tend to overlap since people develop at different rates; some may reach these stages earlier than others.

Early adolescence, from twelve to fourteen years, is important for the development of sexual orientation. According to Sullivan, erotic needs are supposed to be met through the relationship with the opposite gender. The chum, as stated earlier, is a role model of the same sex as the adolescent and with whom the adolescent confides and develops attachment. If one does not make the transition or remains stuck with the chum, one may display homosexual tendencies.[44] The conflicts that the child experiences at this stage are those of sexual gratification, security, and intimacy. Sullivan notes:

> . . .making very much sense of the complexities and difficulties which are experienced in adolescence and subsequent phases of life, depends, in considerable measure, on the clarity with which one distinguishes three needs, which are often very intricately combined and at the same time contradictory. These are the need for personal security-that is, for freedom from anxiety; the need for intimacy-that is, for collaboration with at least one other person; the need for lustful satisfaction, which is connected with genital activity in pursuit of the orgasm.[45]

Late adolescence, from fourteen to eighteen years of age, he says, ". . . extends from the patterning of preferred genital activity through unnumbered educative steps to the establishment of a fully human and

---

43 Ibid., 245ff.

44 Ibid., 277. Sullivan says that there is not enough evidence or "actual facts" to support his theory of sexuality development leading to homosexuality in the adolescent boy. I have not, however, seen any studies countering specifically Sullivan's theory about the development of sexuality.

45 Ibid., 263-264.

mature repertory of interpersonal relations, as permitted by available opportunity, personal and cultural."[46] The late adolescent is discovering his/her "genital behavior and how it fits into the rest of life." He or she continues to learn about how inappropriate and inadequate interpersonal relationships produce anxiety. In other words, s/he is learning about how to minimize anxiety as well as about self-respect and human maturity. There is a realization in the late adolescent that communal existence is important in one's personal identity.[47]

After late adolescence, a person moves on to the final stage, adulthood. The stage of adulthood is one in which a person is expected to have reached maturity. Social expectations allow for a person to marry and have a family. Interpersonal relationships continue to be central in adult life.

One of the key thoughts of Sullivan's developmental theory is that, due to different experiences and interpersonal relationships, a person is transformed. He did not believe that one's personality is set at an early age. In fact, new experiences and new interpersonal relationships can cause changes in one's personality. In other words, one's interpersonal relationships and the amount of anxiety experienced within those relationships affects one's personal identity throughout life. Sullivan says personality is "the relatively enduring pattern of recurrent interpersonal situations which characterize a human life."[48] Interpersonal relationships, which are part of everyday human experiences occurring throughout life, are the basis of the formation of one's personality. The disruption of interpersonal relationships or the lack of a community of embeddedness to foster healthy personal identity development, according to Sullivan, will result in anxiety. In this book, this author is arguing that due to the changes taking place in the urban Shona context, the lack of healthy interpersonal community relations is causing anxiety in individuals' sense of personal identity.

---

46 Ibid., 297.

47 Ibid., 297ff.

48 Sullivan, *Conceptions of Modern Psychiatry*, vi.

As demonstrated throughout the stages of development, the key aspects of Sullivan's theory are interpersonal relations, anxiety, and communal existence. In the urban Shona context, lack of communal existence, interpersonal relationships, and anxiety will be illustrated as the aspects of Sullivan's theory which can give insight to why people seek pastoral care.

General African Personal Identity and the Shona Personal Identity Development. The general African philosophical understanding of a person includes, according to Mbiti, an African theologian from Kenya, "the unborn members who are still in the loins of the living; and the living-dead. . .who are thought to be still interested in the affairs of the family to which they once belonged in their physical life. . .People give offerings of food and libation to the living-dead because they are still part of the family."[49] In other words, the African understanding of a person is not limited to those that are still physically alive but include the dead who are considered as the "living dead."

The key to understanding the person in the African context is community. Without a community of embeddedness, the person is not considered whole. However, without individuals there is no community. Both the individual and the community are integral parts of understanding persons in the African context. Mbiti says the following about the African understanding of person (which includes the Shonas):

> In traditional life, the individual does not and cannot exist alone except corporately. He owes his existence to the other people, including those of past generations and his contemporaries. He is simply part of the whole.
>
> The community must therefore make, create, or produce the individuals, for the individual depends on the corporate group. Physical birth is not enough: the child must go through rites of the incorporation so that it becomes fully integrated into the entire society. These rites continue throughout the physical life of the person, during which the individual passes from one stage of corporate existence to another.[50]

---

49 Mbiti, *African Religions and Philosophy*, 139.

50 Ibid., 141.

Africans traditionally develop an identity or personality through the involvement of the community. The biological influences and personal endowments in the African society are not overlooked. Instead, they are assumed to be present, but alone do not make a person. In the above statement Mbiti underscores that, "physical birth alone is not enough." He goes on further to say,

> Nature brings the child into the world, but society creates the child into the social being, a corporate person. For it is the community which must protect the child, feed it, bring it up, educate it and in many other ways incorporate it into the wider community. Children are buds of society, and every birth is the arrival of'spring' when life shoots out and the community thrives.[51]

The person, or one's personal identity, is believed to be highly influenced by the community or social systems within which one develops. Taking into consideration the biological influences on the concept of a person, the Africans believe that it is the society which gives one an identity or molds one's personality. One is not just a biological entity, but is also a proactive person who reacts to and internalizes the community values and norms in the formation of one's personality.

Mbiti illustrates the importance of the community in individual development when he says, "The individual can only say, 'I am, because we are, since we are, therefore I am.' This is a cardinal point in the understanding of the African view of man."[52] This African philosophical understanding of "person" is quite contrary to Western thought. This is basically because the Western philosophy's understanding of the person emanates from the individual to the society, while the African view is vice versa. Mbiti's statement is equally true in the Shona context; a person is defined within their social context, and in the community. The key to being human therefore lies in interacting within communal interpersonal relationships. Oduyoye, an African woman theologian, suggests this when she notes:

---

51 Ibid.

52 Ibid.

> Africans recognize life as life-in-community. We can truly know ourselves if we remain true to our community, past and present. The concept of individual success or failure is secondary. The ethnic group, the village, the locality, are crucial in one's estimation of oneself. Our nature as beings-in-relation is a two way relation: with God and with our fellow human beings.[53]

Likewise Muzorewa, a Shona theologian, notes the difference between how the West and Africans perceive a person when he says: "Strains of Western thought which have been influenced by Descartes's, 'I think therefore I am,' (cogito ergo sum) and Albert Camus's 'I rebel therefore we exist,' contrast with African concepts of humanity."[54] Muzorewa suggests the Shonas have the community as their starting point in the definition of a person (human) in contrast to the West's individual as a starting point. All the authors, Oduyoye, Muzorewa, and Mbiti, address the importance of community in the development of an individual as a person. It is important to examine how the traditional Shona context did understand communal interpersonal relationships of personal identity. Only then can we examine the anxiety created in the Shona context as a result of the influence of Westernization.

Shona Personal Identity Development. Little has been written from the Shona context tracing the stages of personal identity development. Due to lack of written material from the Shona context tracing stages of personal identity development, I will depend mainly on two different books, one written by Gelfand and another edited by Mutswairo.[55] Gelfand was a

---

53 Mercy A. Oduyoye, "The Value of African Religious Beliefs and Practices for Christian Theology," in K. Appiah-Kubi and S. Torres, eds., *African Theology En Route* (New York: Maryknoll, Orbis Books, 1979), 100-101.

54 Gwinyai H. Muzorewa, *The Origins and Development of African Theology* (New York: Maryknoll, Orbis Books, 1985), 30-34.

55 M. Gelfand, *Growing up in a Shona Society* (Gweru: Mambo Press, 1979). In this book Gelfand presented how children grow up in the Shona context. To test the impact of the change taking place in urban areas, he did research in different schools in Harare. He also researched how the children who were being raised in the cities were learning about the traditional culture and life in the rural areas. Some of Gelfand's findings were issues of "bi-culturalism" or of children raised in the cities, not being able to "fit in" in

was a medical doctor and writer who taught at the then University of Rhodesia starting from about the 1960s. The editor Mutswairo, currently Professor at the University of Zimbabwe in the Department of African Languages and Literature, specializes in Traditional Oral Literature in Africa. Based on the lack of sufficient material, the author will also use relevant written material from other African contexts and some personal experiences which illustrate the Shona traditional situations.

The belief of the traditional Shonas notes that the individual exists because of the community; however, the community cannot be without individuals. In this book, I am not focusing on the debate of individual versus community rights; rather, the concern is about the involvement of the community in the molding of the individual and the development of a personal identity. A person attains personhood through socialization, passing on of communal beliefs, values, norms, and mores. One cannot claim to "be" without the community. The Shona saying, *Munhu vanhu,* which means a person is because of other people, illustrates that individual identity depends on the corporate community. The values, beliefs, and norms an individual internalizes from the community are those which help one formulate individual identity. The community supplies or equips individuals with the things necessary for identity development. One of the main focuses of this book is to show how communal interpersonal relationships are key to the personal identity development in Sullivan's theory and the traditional Shona context. Lack of these interpersonal relationships, as posited by Sullivan, causes anxiety, and can be detected in the urban Shona context today.

Having stated the influences of communal interpersonal relationships in personal identity, I will present the traditional Shona stages of personal identity development, mainly drawing on Gelfand and Masasire. The late Masasire, who was teaching at the University of Zimbabwe in the Department of African Languages and Literature, contributed a chapter focused on issues of growing up in the traditional Shona context in the

---

rural area settings. See also Solomon Mutswairo ed., *Introduction to the Shona Culture* (Kadoma: Juta Zimbabwe Pvt. Ltd., 1996), 44-62. Traces development and training from conception to adulthood.

book edited by Mutswairo.[56] Relevant material from Mbiti's writing will also be utilized.

In traditional Shona culture, from the moment a woman realizes she is pregnant she goes to the elderly women of the community who know about the herbs and the charms the pregnant mother is supposed have. The mother takes herbs and wears protective charms to prevent harm to the fetus. In some Shona communities, sex between husband and wife will cease when the mother is in her final month of pregnancy. A pregnant woman is held with respect and not allowed to overwork in case harm may occur to the life of both the mother and fetus. As Masasire illustrates:

> During pregnancy the wife continues with her normal activities, although she may discontinue heavier work in the later months. Many taboos and avoidances must be observed by pregnant women, usually to protect the child, but sometimes, also to ease the pregnancy and labor. . .Women are often given medicines during pregnancy to relieve the pains and sickness, to facilitate the birth or to protect the foetus against harm *(mishonga yamasuo)*.[57]

Naturally, following pregnancy comes the birth of the baby. The next section covers the period up to five years of age. The cutting of the umbilical cord is of significance to the Shona in that it is a sign of separation of the baby from the mother. In most cases, the umbilical cord is disposed of by burying it. The child is separate from the mother but is also in close proximity to the mother. According to Masasire:

> The cord is cut at birth, and then after birth is buried secretly to prevent strangers or witches from tampering with and causing harm to the child. The infant is washed and often given a little porridge, or medical infusion soon after being born. For some time after birth, the baby is believed to be very weak and rituals may be performed to strengthen and protect it. The rituals link the new member to the whole family. The mother and the infant remain secluded in the hut for a period varying between six days and ten days.[58]

---

56 Albert Masasire, "Kinship and Marriage," 46.

57 Ibid., 46.

58 Ibid., 45.

During the time of seclusion, the involvement of the midwife, and in many cases the grandmother, is now a sign that the baby no longer belongs to the mother only but to the whole community. At the end of the six to ten days of seclusion of the mother, baby, grandmother, and midwife, the cord is expected to separate from the navel, *kudonha chikuvhu*.

A ceremony is performed which in some cases combines with the naming ceremony called *kubudisa mwana* (meaning "bringing the child out to the community"). The child is named and given or presented to the community to raise. In other communities, the child is named and then a ceremony of presenting the child to the community is done. The name one is given at birth or in infancy, in most Shona communities, has a meaning. In most cases the name is connected to, or describes the personality or character of, the child. Sometimes the name may be descriptive of the family's relationship with relatives or others in the community or related to a crucial event surrounding the pregnancy or birth of the child. The name of the child might also be symbolic of what is perceived as the quality of the child's character or personality. Mbiti says about the incorporation of a child into the community:

> The child has, however, begun its journey of being incorporated into the community, so that the separation between the individual mother and child continues to widen as the child's integration into the wider community also increases. . .Paradoxically, then, the child is near the mother and yet begins to get away from the individual mother, growing into the status of being 'I am because we are and since we are therefore I am'. . .the child is now public property, it belongs to the entire community and is no longer the property of one person. It has died to the stage of being alone in the mother's womb: but now it has risen in the new life of being part of the human society.[59]

It is no longer the sole responsibility of the immediate family to raise the child but the responsibility of the community. The belief that "It takes a village to raise a child" is also prevalent among the traditional Shonas.

In most communities the child is allowed to breast feed until about the age of two. The following, of what Mbiti says, is true of the Shona context: "During the nursing period, the child is carried on the back or bosom of the

59 Mbiti, *African Religions and Philosophy*, 147-148.

mother or of another female member of the village. The direct contact between the mother and child gives the child a deep psychological sense of security."[60] The task of carrying the baby is also shared by the older sisters, cousins, grandmothers, and aunts. As the baby grows older, it starts to realize that it does not belong to the mother alone but develops attachment with others (community).

Until the age of two to two-and-a-half years the child still sleeps with the parents. The child is expected to acquire a language, walk, and be toilet trained by the end of five years. Among the Shonas, the end of this phase and the beginning of the next may overlap since these phases are arbitrary and may be attained at different rates by each child. Toward the end of this stage the child is starting to sleep with children of the same sex as him/herself or of the same age, separate from the parents.

During the ages of about six to twelve, the community starts training the child about community expectations and responsibilities. Gelfand, basing his information from the traditional Shona context, notes:

> At this stage the children no longer sleep in the same room as their parents, they are taught the difference between good behavior and bad behavior and they also learn to avoid a number of taboos. . .If they sit on the road they will develop boils on their buttocks. They may meet a lion if they walk backwards. Peeping toms will develop sties,. . .Dust must not be swept out of the hut at night. . .Children are forbidden to whistle or call at night lest they attract witches.[61]

With the aid of and training by older siblings, the child starts to look after the family animals and sometimes those of the extended family. The child is starting to learn responsibility, even though he or she is not considered a mature person. The taking of duties similar to those of adults gives the children the sense that they are passing through the stage of being a baby to another stage of childhood where the child is responsible to the community.

The boys at this stage are expected to learn to take care of the animals, make and use weapons, help weed the fields, water the gardens, and feed

---

60 Ibid., 156.

61 Gelfand, *Growing up in a Shona Society*, 12-13.

the chickens and their dogs. Toward the end of this phase, the boys sit outside in the open air, a place around the fire, *kudare*, where the elderly men teach the young people about life and being a responsible communal human being. The women stay inside the house with the girls and do the same. Girls at this age start to learn about cooking, cleaning the house, and taking care of younger siblings. Stories using animal characters (such as the baboon, hare, lion, hyena, etc.) are told at this phase to emphasize good character, language, and manners.

The children are taught a lot of proverbs, riddles, and stories to help them learn to be responsible people in the community and to build character. This is a time when children are corrected in the presence of others so that others may learn from the mistakes of some. They are taught about taboos. A taboo is a prohibited, restricted, or forbidden behavior. If someone is to commit such an act (taboo), he or she receives automatic consequences through natural laws, the spirits, or God. The children are taught the importance of maintaining good interpersonal relations, with animal stories as illustrations. Good interpersonal relationships must be maintained with others in order for harmony to exist.

What the children are taught by their grandparents, aunts, uncles, or elders of the family is constantly reinforced in the community. Any elderly person can discipline any child in the community if a child is found misbehaving. The reinforcement of values, norms, and character building also happens in the in-groups of the girls or boys. They remind each other of the taboos since most of the taboos will affect not only the one who breaks them but the whole family or community as well. One is said to be developing a good *unhu* (character or personhood); for example, having respect for the elders (*ano kudza vakuru wake*), or *kutumika,* which means being sent and doing it ungrudgingly. In addition, children must not use bad words or language, learn to ask questions about things of which they are unsure, admit when they are wrong, and be helpful to strangers. Having a good relationship or being helpful to a stranger is a way of creating harmony with that stranger's community. The stranger will spread news to his/her community of the hospitality given him or her at a time he/she needed it, rather than vice-versa.

This is the point at which the children are taught proverbs such as, *Varume ndevamwe, kutsva kwendebvu vanodzimurana*. Hamutyinei, a Shona literature writer, translates the proverb:

> (Men should show a spirit of cooperation and sympathy. They should help one another in times of difficulty and danger). At times, this proverb is quoted as an encouragement to work together. It also serves as a reproach for people who are reluctant to give a hand to those who need it.[62]

Another proverb which would apply to respecting people regardless of, for example, one's disabilities is, *Munhu, Munhu asina kubarwa ndiyani*? which translates as, "A person is a person, is there one who was not given birth to?" *Munhu vanhu* (a person is because of others) also teaches the child that s/he is because of others or the community, without which s/he ceases to *be*.

As Gelfand says, the next arbitrary phase extends from about twelve to eighteen years of age. Among the Shonas, this phase includes the physical and/or mental developmental changes in the child. Girls develop breasts and they have their menstruation. Boys develop deeper voices, pubic hair, and sometimes they experience their first ejaculation. This is a period in which the aunts, uncles, or grandparents do a lot of work to educate the adolescents about adulthood. The education is mostly done during the evenings. Usually the boys and girls in this age group are separated, but sometimes they are taken together and given a series of lessons about manhood and womanhood. Boys in the early part of adolescence are known as *kajaya* and girls are known as *kamhandara*. At the late part of this phase (18 years old), a boy is *jaya* and girl *mhandara*, which is adolescent. Both boys and girls are taught about sexual relationships. Sexual intercourse before marriage is highly discouraged. This is a period where *kuzvibata* (self-control, self-respect) is emphasized and tested. One might hear statements being used, such as *mwana asina hunhu*, meaning "a child without character or having bad behavior." The implication of this is that the child is developing a bad personality, and the saying can be used when a child is being disrespectful of his or her elders.

---

62 M. A. Hamutyinei, *Tsumo Namadimikira* (Gweru: Mambo Press, 1984), 39.

Gelfand gives the following list of things girls are to learn at this age: "The girls are taught how to take care of children, use of clean language, cleanliness, temper control, how to react to courting proposals, and how to relate to one's in-laws."[63] For girls, one would hear proverbs such as *musha mukadzi*, which translates as "a stable home is because of the wife." The training regarding marriage, procreation, sexual life, family responsibilities, allowance of full privileges, and duties to the community occur in the context of the home. The aunts, uncles, and grandparents act as mentors to this age group until its members are ready for marriage.

There are times when elders in the community, who are not necessarily related to the boys or girls by blood, would provide the same educational duties in their homes. In some traditional Shona communities this is the time when the initiation ceremony, which includes circumcision, takes place. Again, the things which adolescents are taught are constantly reinforced by any of the adults or elders of the community, especially those of the same sex as the adolescent. Similar to Sullivan's theory, these elders act as chums.

The next stage is that of marriage and procreation. One goes through the period of courtship. When ready to be married, a man must have accumulated some money or gifts to give to the family of the bride (bride wealth/ dowry). If the man has brothers, they would also contribute towards the dowry. A woman is married into a family; a man likewise marries into a family. Marriage is not just the union of two individuals, but the uniting of two families. It is a rare case in the Shona traditional culture in which marriage is an agreement only between two people, without the involvement of the families or community. Marriage makes one creative and reproductive. The children born to the marriage become the link between the parents in the marital relationship, the extended families, and with the departed (the past) and the generations to come (the future). This is also a period in which one engages in the responsibility of family and becomes a senior to all those who are unmarried (younger adults) of the community. One assumes leadership positions in the community (mentoring/ apprenticing younger members of the community), advocates

---

63 Gelfand, *Growing up in a Shona Society*, 27.

for good communal interpersonal relationships, and makes decisions on behalf of one's family.

As one grows older in wisdom, character, wise counsel, and experience, one is elevated to eldership in the community. In many communities there are no rituals connected to this stage. With experience and age, one is believed to attain the position of elder. One of the key roles of the elder is to make sure healthy interpersonal relationships are maintained within the family or the community.

Before presenting how Sullivan's theory would help inform the pastoral caregiver in the urban Shona context that is in transition, it is important to note the changes caused by Westernization. Again, the lack of communal interpersonal relations deemed central in both Sullivan's theory and the traditional Shona culture (village setting) has become a source of anxiety for the urban Shona people, requiring pastoral caregivers with an integrative consciousness to serve in this context.

Personal Identity in the Contemporary Urban Shona Context. The advent of urbanization and Westernization upset the traditional village structure. Bourdillon (who has written much about the Shona), Gelfand, and Mbiti note that urbanization changed the traditional cultural and religious ways of life. The urban setting does not encourage communal living. Most of the upper middle class families in the city have both parents working outside the home. The mothers leave their babies early to return to work, and the infants and children are then raised by house maids. Remember that, according to Sullivan's findings, the mother's consistent absence can produce anxiety or a "not me" personality in the infant. The situation has changed from the traditional context in which the mother was present, nursing, and carrying the baby for up to the age of about two years.

These house maids are mostly teenagers themselves, who are not well vested in the Shona traditional culture or moral values. Some of the house maids are still probing their own identity or sexuality about which no one might have educated them; they therefore lack the wisdom with which to teach the children of the household about adulthood. Because of the fast-pace of life in the cities, some parents do not have the time to teach their children about life and sexuality; instead the television movies inform children before the parents do. There is lack of adult supervision since both parents are working. Masasire notes about the impact of change in the urban setting:

> Much of the success of traditional methods of socialization rested on the homogeneity and relatively static nature of society. With the accelerating rate of change in these societies [urban Shona] today, child-rearing techniques have gone through many changes.[64]

The setting in the cities is different from the traditional villages in which any adult could discipline the youth. In the cities, the children are under no obligation to listen to a stranger. Life in the cities is based on competition, not cooperation. The children are without the luxury of having elders to train them about adulthood in the traditional sense; therefore some children grow up without personal role models who could act as "chums" for them. The substitute role model they have might be an actor, singer, etc., on the television, for example, Michael Jordan or Tupac, with whom they may never have a personal relationship.

Kapenzi, a Shona, writing on the clash of cultures in the Shona context, says,

> Conflicts between the old and the new social principles are producing new rivalries unknown in the traditional tribal order. Industrialization and urbanization have released new forces and created new groups. Members of a family are isolated more and more from each other. Men and women are taken far away out of their families and kinship groups, where they become involved with strangers within a whole system of impersonal institutions.[65]

Kapenzi's argument on the cultural clash is quite apparent in the urban context today and this is what sets the Shonas in a personal identity conflict. In the cities, kinship such as that in the village setting is no longer primary. Having small families is being encouraged in the name of economic feasibility.

---

64 Masasire, "Kinship and Marriage," 45.

65 Geoffrey Z. Kapenzi, *The Clash of Cultures: Christian Missionaries and the Shona of Rhodesia (now Zimbabwe)* (Washington D.C.: University Press of America, 1979), 47.

In their research on the Zimbabwean cities (mostly Harare), both Gelfand (cited in Chapter One) and Bourdillon found that most urban parents try to have their children educated about the traditional Shona culture by sending the children to the rural areas.[66] However, this has proven ineffective since the children have the tendency to perceive rural life as backward. In turn, the rural folks, especially the elders, look at these city children as modernized and lacking an understanding of or respect for the Shona traditional life, morals, values, and culture. Bourdillon notes:

> One result of the weakening links between parents and children, and between children and traditional society, is that people born and brought up in town often do not know how to behave correctly when they visit their relatives in the country. They have not learnt the details of traditional social patterns. . .Besides, they are likely to have a higher standard of living than the rural kin and children in the towns are more aware of wealth differentials than absent patterns of kinship: parents of such children may find it difficult to persuade them to pay due respect to rural elders which may involve sitting on the ground soiling their smart town clothes.[67]

Most children growing up in the cities are of the opinion that the traditional beliefs are oppressive and backward. Mbiti also argues that the cultural change, taking place in the African context in general, is producing "half-cultured people." He notes,

> Modern change tries to plant a form of culture which is shallow at least on the African soil. It is a culture of the alphabet and comics, of pop music and transistor television and magazines with pictures of semi-naked women, of individualism and economic competition, of mass production and ever accelerating speed of life. Men and women are forced to live in two half cultures which do not unite to form one culture.[68]

The point Mbiti is making is similar to the one argued earlier about the contemporary urban Shonas lacking a culture which can provide the

---

66 Michael Bourdillon, *The Shona Peoples*, rev. ed. (Gweru: Mambo Press, 1991), 311-330; see also Gelfand, *Growing up in a Shona Society*, chap. 2 and 4 passim.

67 Ibid., 318.

68 Mbiti, *African Religions and Philosophy*, 288-289.

children and youth with a strong foundation. The church has not prepared pastoral caregivers serving the urban generations for helping them to handle the changes taking place in these people's lives, and the Western culture is not a legitimate substitute for the traditional culture. The urban culture places more emphasis on the individual, and the training of boys and girls, a task which used to be given in the traditional Shona culture, is no longer available or is perceived as not suitable for the urban context.

Some parents in the urban areas are uncomfortable talking to or teaching their own children about sexual matters since this was the aunts', uncles', and grandparents' role. These people (aunts, uncles, etc.) are not readily available in the cities. At the same time, there is no one else to teach their children about sexual issues except for the television and popular sexually explicit lyrics heard over the radio. In such a setting, the children end in confusion about developing a personal identity; there is no one to provide structure and accountability as there was in the traditional context. The education, which is provided by foreign Western culture through the media (emphasizing I, me, my, and mine), is not fully understood either.

In the cities, children do not have to live by the traditional rules such as respect of one's elders, respect of the community values and morals, believing the common African world-view such as, "I am therefore we are, since we are therefore I am," or "One tree does not make a forest." Anxiety strikes when the adult or the child growing up in the city realizes that s/he does not have a community support system founded in interpersonal relations. The children growing up in the city realize the lack of communal support and do not have that sense of community internalized or ingrained in them because the ways in which they were brought up are individualistic. Anxiety also arises primarily when the child realizes a lack of community support and has to deal with relatives who live in the village setting where there is that sense of communal support. The traditional Shona society's stages of development have no place or are not regarded in the urban context. The Western individualistic educational system plus the media have replaced the traditional educational systems without providing all the benefits of the traditional society.

The Missing Link in the Urban Shona Setting. The missing link for the urban population, in line with Sullivan's theory of interpersonal relationships and communal existence, is the lack of a sense of connectedness or communal interrelatedness. People are connected to their wealth more than their interpersonal relationships. The children growing up in such a context tend to internalize economic values of competition more than kinship values. One lives a life of competition more than of harmony. The idea of "I" is valued more than that of "we." Having grown up with an individualistic mode of life, the children find that non-communal frame of reference detrimental when they ask the questions regarding one's identity, the relational connectedness of one's roots, and one's history and origins.

I agree with the conclusion reached by Mwikamba, a Catholic priest as well as a lecturer in the Department of Religious Studies at Nairobi University. He notes:

> . . .it is clear that the Western identity and the African identity differ, and that they have different emphases. Friendship, solidarity, respect for nature, respect for human dignity, the right relationship within community and extended family, which includes both the living and dead, are values regarded with high esteem in African traditional society. However, these values seem to be fading away from 'modern' African society.
>
> Many of the so called 'modern' Africans are strangers to themselves, to other people and to nature. The harmonious and symbiotic relationship between a person and the object, between a person and the world, seem to be breaking down. In the past, the symbiotic relationships made an African world of experience to be personal, for the world could not be separated from the self. The self could not be separated from other people or from the world; and all of them could not be separated from God.[69]

The upper middle class urban Shonas are ashamed to go back to the "backward" way of life to get their sense of personal identity, and at the same time they find that having chosen a life of individualism has led them to living a lonely life. Their personal identity is based on their economic possessions and not on interpersonal relationships. The analysis of cases in

---

69 Constantine M. Mwikamba, "A Search for an African Identity," *AFER African Ecclesial Review* 31 (February, 1989): 99-100.

Chapter Five helps clarify the issues raised in this chapter with regards to personal identity confusion.

When anxiety sets in, those who belong to Christian families may choose to go to their pastors for help, as will be demonstrated in the next chapter and by the case studies in Chapter Five. This author agrees with Sullivan that anxiety is one of the main reasons why people seek help, including in the Shona context, when interpersonal relations are ignored:

> . . .it is necessary to appreciate that it is anxiety which is responsible for a great part of the inadequate, inefficient, unduly rigid, or otherwise unfortunate performances of people; that anxiety is responsible in a basic sense for a great deal of what comes to a psychiatrist for attention.[70]

There are many reasons why people need help, as stated above by Sullivan; however, Sullivan also believes that faulty interpersonal relations, or threats to one's security or personal identity, are other ways in which people become anxious. A pastor with an integrative consciousness who is cognizant of the Shona traditional culture, the Western culture, and/or the integration thereof, is equipped to help youth or individuals going through such a personal identity crisis. Sullivan's theory provides a pastoral caregiver reasons to explore issues of interpersonal relationships and communal existence which might be causing anxiety to those living in the urban Shona context and a theoretical framework within which to do so. For the Shona there is also the spiritual or religious aspect of being involved in interpersonal relationships to assure personal wholeness.

The next chapter explores the issues of interpersonal relationships, anxiety, communal existence in traditional Shona context, in relationship to their religion and theology, and the lack of this in the contemporary urban Shona religion. The focus is on the Shona relational theology or the importance of interpersonal relations in their religious world-view and theology.

---

70 Sullivan, *Interpersonal Theory of Psychiatry*, 160.

CHAPTER FOUR
Traditional Shona Relational Theology

Hukama, which translates as kinship "relations by blood or marriage," and also sometimes translates as one's "interpersonal relationships," is one of the key elements tying the Shona communities together. This concept influences the world-view of these communities, particularly how they perceive life and being human. *Hukama* signifies many facets of one's relational interconnectedness, affiliations, interdependence, communal existence, ties to one's family and community, and integration of these factors into one's being. In addition, the concept of *hukama* is central to how the Shona relate to God and the Spirit World. Illustrative of this centrality is the Shona saying *Hukama hwakanaka hunopfuura hupfumi*, which literally means "having strong relationships is better than being wealthy." This saying is common among the Shona. For the Shona, a person who has good interpersonal relationships can rely on the support of his or her relatives, instead of having to rely on one's wealth in times of need. Thus, in the Shona world-view, one's interpersonal relationships are of great value to one's sense of being. The goal of this chapter is an attempt to demonstrate that communal interpersonal relations between God, humans, and nature, in the traditional Shona society, are predicated on religion. For instance, the way to relate with creation, such as land and trees, is based on traditional Shona religious understanding.

I find Sullivan's theory on communal interpersonal relations compatible to the traditional Shona understanding of relationships. However, Sullivan's argument that humans are born with "an instinct to relate" (the basis of his theory of interpersonal relations) is partially illuminating to traditional Shona understanding of the urge to relate. In this theory, one finds that Sullivan puts emphasis on the relationship rather than the instinct itself. I view Sullivan's use of the concept of instinct as one that refers to aspects of an instinct that are not biologically based, but one that views instincts as tendencies or inclinations toward the need to relate. As a result, Sullivan's theory is that of interpersonal relations and communal existence based on his understanding of the human tendencies or inclinations to relate.

I agree with Sullivan's notion of the human tendencies or inclinations to relate to others beginning from infancy, including the need to be in relationship with creation, for survival. However, what Sullivan's theory of communal interpersonal relationships does not adequately address is the spiritual (religious, God, or Spirit World) aspect of interpersonal relationships in human beings. Sullivan discusses human-to-human and human-to-creation relationships, but nothing is stated about humans and their relationship with God.

Instinct to Relate in Traditional Shona Religion

I add that there is in the traditional African religio-culture, and more specifically for the traditional Shona people, the recognition of the spiritual or religious aspects to "the human instinct to relate."[1] For the traditional Shonas, this "human instinct to relate to an outside power" is not argued as one that is limited to the Shonas only; but that the way to understanding how humans relate to God is readily recognized as such in the traditional African society. One of the key aspects to indicate the difference between the West and the traditional African context is the presence of formal instructional structures (Sunday School) to teaches children about religion in the West, and the lack of such structures in the traditional African or

1 The author realizes that the word instinct has been used in many negative ways against the African people. There are dangers in using the word in that one could read the author's use of the concept instinct as reducing the traditional Shona religion to an instinct. Religion as an instinct is not defining the religion in and of itself, but the tendencies or inclinations people have in becoming religious. The words "to relate" qualifying the word instinct are central to the use of this concept.

Shona societies. Thus religion becomes "folk knowledge," practiced through participation and observation.

There is in the traditional Shona understanding a "spiritual instinct to relate" to a power outside of oneself, such as relating to *Musiki* (the Creator) or *Mwari*–(God), and the Spirit World. Moyo, a former professor at the University of Zimbabwe, without using the word "instinct" in describing traditional African religion, implicates it:

> In African traditional thought, religion is not just another aspect of the culture but something inseparable from it: a way of life which embraces all aspects of human relations. Zimbabwean traditional thought cannot conceive of a human being without religion and without participation in the life, beliefs and practices of the community. Religion and culture are as it is were interchangeable. No African language of which I am aware, particularly in southern Africa, has a word equivalent to the English term "religion." The idea of such a thing, isolated from the rest of life and practiced on its own, does not exist. In the holistic worldview characteristic of all Africa, there can be no separation between the sacred and the profane, the spiritual and the material. Religion interweaves everything; hence, asking an African "What is your religion?" is like asking "What is your way of life?"[2]

Setiloane, even though writing from the South African context about African theology, wrote a subsection entitled "Religion as an Instinct" in addressing his understanding of African religion for the African people:

> The three seem to fall upon him/her all at the same time: Consciousness of self, consciousness of the community of humans and animals, and consciousness of Divinity as the Cause of being. So like the sense of being human or the sense of community, religion, a sense of a Power other than self, at work and determining existence, its origins and vicissitudes, is not something acquired. It is as old as being human itself; it is of the human's very nature. Hence the difference between Africa and the West in their attitude towards religion. There is actually no African word to translate 'religion.' At best it is translated as 'a people's ways' or 'customs' (mekgwa/amasiko) something lived and practiced, not discussed and discoursed about.[3]

---

2 Ambrose Moyo, *Zimbabwe: The Risk of Incarnation* (Gospel and Culture series Switzerland: World Council of Churches, 1996), 1-2.

3 Gabriel Setiloane, *African Theology: An Introduction* (Johannesburg: Skotaville Publishers, 1986), 41.

Setiloane is arguing that the sense of relating to an outside power, outside of the self, is one which is part of human nature. The main idea I borrow from Setiloane is the fact that religion for the Africans is something which is practiced and lived; it is a way of life. As instinct, it is part of the human inclinations and tendencies to relate to a power outside of themselves, present from the time of infancy. I add that as one grows older, the tendencies or inclinations to relate to God increase through living and practicing. This missing piece in Sullivan's theory of the "spiritual instinct to relate" is what I am using, as a way to introduce the chapter in presenting the importance of communal interpersonal relations.

Defining Traditional Shona Relational Theology

The advent of Western Christianity, and the condemnation of traditional Shona religion by Western Christianity, resulted in limiting some of the relational theological grounding on which the urban contemporary Shona pastoral caregiver can draw. What is relational theology from the traditional Shona context? How does it differ from other relational theologies? The Shona relational theology is informed by the traditional communal religio-cultural values of the Shona traditional society. As aforementioned, these values are grounded upon one's relationships with God, humans, and nature through the community. The redemptive plan of Shona relational theology is holistic rather than individualistic. In traditional Shona society, it is through relating to God, others and nature that one gets a sense of the spiritual self.

There are different types of Western relational theologies. One of the fundamental values of Western Christianity is the belief of maintaining a relationship with the One Supreme Being, God. However, the one God is holistic in three persons: Father, Son, and the Holy Spirit. Christians, however, do not relate to the three as different entities but as One being (Trinitarian theology). Then, there is also eco-theology which focuses on human relationship with creation or nature.[4] Another type of theology is anthrolopological theology which emphasizes human nature, destiny, and

4 Larry L. Rasmussen, *Earth Community, Earth Ethic* New York: Orbis Books, Maryknoll, 1996.

human relations to the divine. In these other relational theologies, the relationships are not equally balanced, while in the traditional Shona relational theology, all the elements (nature, humans, Spirit World), are equally interdependent. What affects nature affects humanity, what affects humanity affects the Spirit World, and vice versa. The traditional Shona relational theology is one that seeks equilibrium in all of the relationships. Failure in any of the relationships produces a "domino effect" on the other relationships, resulting in disequilibrium.

Relationships and Rituals in Traditional Shona Society. Rituals and relationships are central in religious beliefs and customs of the Shonas. Rituals are believed to be a means to right the wrong caused by faulty relationships. In the traditional Shona context, interpersonal relations take the form of interaction, relatedness, interdependence, or interconnectedness between "one" and the "other." The "one" or the "other" may refer to humans, nature, God, or Spiritual beings. The words "interpersonal relations" and "relationships" are used interchangeably since they draw the same meanings for this book. A key assertion in this chapter is what Maimela, a South African theologian, suggests about relationships and rituals in the African context:

> Africans are taught and expected to engage themselves in those activities that will enhance the total welfare of the community of which they are a part by: (a) avoiding bad relationships with those among whom the individual lives so as to make self-fulfilment in life by all those concerned possible; (b) engaging in various religious rites which maintain the well-being of the community, because failure to comply with them will release evil forces that will bring illness or misfortune of one kind or another.[5]

Maimela's claim is central to many traditional Africans including the Shona people. Rituals become a main avenue by which relationships between humans, creation, and the Spirit World are maintained, hence, their importance for consideration in this book.

Malidoma Some, from Burkina Faso, in writing about form and function of ritual among the African communities, summarizes it well:

---

5 S. Maimela, "Salvation in African Traditional Religions," *Missionalia* 13, No. 2, (Aug 1985): 67.

> Ritual is by its nature a communal activity and an act of creation. The people involved must develop these details themselves to fit the particular need that is being addressed. The ritual must create a certain kind of energy that can embrace individuals involved, allowing them to expand their awareness and undergo the transformation necessary to become healed. . .Ritual, community, and healing-these three are so intertwined in the indigenous world that to speak of one of them is to speak of them all. *Ritual*, communally designed, helps the individual remember his or her purpose, such remembering brings healing both to the individual and the community. The *community* exists, in part, to safeguard the purpose of each person within it. . .*Healing* comes when the individual remembers his or her identity-the purpose chosen in the world of ancestral wisdom-and reconnects with that world of Spirit. Human beings long for connection, and our sense of usefulness derives from the feeling of connectedness. When we are connected-to our own purpose, to the community around us, and to our spiritual wisdom-we are able to live and act with authentic effectiveness.[6]

The meaning and function of ritual described above by Some is the same as found in the traditional Shona context. The purpose of ritual is to transform and bring healing to dysfunctional interpersonal relations.

It is not unusual to hear Shonas say: *Ida hama dzako, mombe haikuchengeti,* which translates as, "Love or be in good relationship with your relatives for a cow (a symbol of one's possessions or wealth) won't take care of you." Even if one had the money to go to the most expensive doctors, the idea is that one still needs relational support. For example, only one's relatives can accord a person proper burial if one dies. If one is not accorded a proper burial, one's spirit wanders around. One has to be accorded the full burial ritual to become an ancestor or join the community of the Spirit World. The worst thing that can happen to a deceased person's spirit, or to a living human being, in the Shona context is to be cut off from the Spirit World or one's community respectively, since one's personal identity is based in one's community of embeddedness.

While relationships are valued more than wealth, being wealthy is not evil. However, people are expected to share their riches with those in need within the family or community. Sharing is not only the right thing to do, it is also believed that the sharing of one's wealth with the poor or others strengthens relationships and is a sign of a good communal spirit. Another

---

6 Malidoma Patrice Some, *The Healing Wisdom of Africa: Finding Life Purpose Through Nature, Ritual and Community* (New York: Penguin Putnam Inc.), 1998, 35-36.

saying among the Shona, *Hukama igaswa, hunozadziswa nekudya*, translates as, "a relationship is only partial until one shares a meal with the other." Illustrative of this belief is that in any reconciling ritual or ceremony, the two reconciling parties/families must prepare a meal together and share the meal in order to seal the conciliation or the new relationship. In these ceremonies, the ancestors and God are also involved as libation is poured out and some of the food is offered to them. Through the ancestors, the name of God is invoked as part of the ceremony and peace meal. The process of reconciliation is important in relationships because it functions as a seal of reparation for past broken relationships. Rituals repair shattered relationships, bridging them to renewed healthy relational beginnings. When relationships become broken, rituals are performed to bring the community to equilibrium. Maimela also says of the African society in general, in terms of rituals:

> In order to help save people from anxieties that are experienced due to life's contingencies, from the vagaries of nature, from potential impotency, from bad luck and from the malevolent spirits, witches and sorcerers, the African Traditional Religions have designed a variety of protective rites and rituals. . . Furthermore, there are purificatory rites to cleanse those who are defiled so as to avoid impending destruction of the individual concerned as well as the threatening of the well-being of one's corporate existence. In addition, a variety of sacrificial offerings have been developed over the years to atone for whatever wrong or sin an individual or the community might have committed. [7]

Maimela echoes the fact that rituals, rites, and sacrifices are key to how Africans maintain their relationship with God. God is experienced in terms of interpersonal relationships, which is the Shona community's core of existence. Re-evaluating rituals and rites in the church offers the opportunity to integrate and reclaim some of the traditional religious practices inasmuch as rituals play such a central role in interpersonal relationships and in the Shona world-view. There is the need for rituals to be essentially cooperative and communal rather than individualistic in their function.

Sacrifices and rituals are thus means by which order is restored. There is a ritual for almost every little thing, performed so as not to disrupt life in

7 Maimela, "Salvation in African Traditional Religions," 69-70.

relationship with God and the "other." Thus, most of the missionaries, when observing life in African communities, said the people were "notoriously religious."[8] Partly, the religiousness of the African communities is due to the need for maintaining their relationship with God, which is also a sign of humanity's dependence on God.

Interpersonal Relationships: Humans, God and Nature. Muzorewa, a Shona theologian, suggests that strife in relationships between humans, and between humans and God or creation, is perceived as the main cause or source of tension in the Shona communities. Chaos and catastrophes may occur when there is violation of the customs, mores, and religious ways of the community. Muzorewa further notes:

> So, we find that African humanity is primarily defined by a sense of belonging, serving one's own folk, and kinship. For the African, it is not enough to be a human being; unless one shares a sense of community, one can easily turn out to be an enemy. . .African theology may derive the criteria for belonging to a community of believers from this traditional concept of humanity in community. Such a definition of the community of believers takes collective survival very seriously. [9]

Here, Muzorewa addresses the importance of community and how African traditional religious culture may influence contemporary African theology. What Muzorewa is saying is in line with I understand of the significance of communal interpersonal relations in the traditional context. Some of the traditional understandings of communal relations need to be utilized in the Shona pastoral theology of care today.

A pastoral care-giver with an integrative consciousness must understand the importance and primacy of interpersonal relationships in the traditional Shona world-view, e.g. myths, rituals, etc. At times, the traditional Shona understanding of interpersonal relations contradicts that of Christianity in that the Shona understanding may include rituals which call for peace making with creation, for which the Shona Christian rituals now in place do not provide.

---

8 Mbiti, *African Religions and Philosophy*, 1.

9 Muzorewa, *The Origins and Development*, 17.

God and Humanity, and the Shona Myths. In the traditional Shona context, humanity was believed to have been created to be in relationship with God. Without a relationship with God, the community and its meaning ceases. In other words, in the Shona traditional society, the community cannot exist wholly or without chaos in the absence of being in relationship with God. In addition, interpersonal human relations affect the individual's relationship with God. What an individual does in terms of one's relationship with God affects the family or community just as much as the community's actions affect the individual's relationship with God. For example, according to the traditional Shona beliefs, when an individual murders someone, it will not only affect the individual's relationship with God, but will also affect the entire family's relationship with the family of the deceased and with God for generations to come, until the time of reconciliation.

The entire family and sometimes the community in the traditional Shona society will need cleansing and forgiveness from God for acts of murder yet to be pardoned. The rituals performed are not just for the sake of the individual involved but include the entire community. Murphree talks about the belief of the Shona people, that acts such as incest or any other act contrary to the laws of *Mwari* (God) are punishable by God, who sends lightning as a punishment to the offenders.[10] Murphree is pointing to the communal responsibility aspect. Mbiti says the following about the African communities' beliefs and understanding of their relationship to God and one another:

> Beliefs are expressed through concepts of God, attitudes towards him, and the various acts of worship. Furthermore, they are collective, communal, or corporate beliefs, held by groups or communities. The individual 'believes' what other members of the corporate society 'believe,' and he 'believes' because others 'believe.'[11]

---

10 Marshall W. Murphree, *Christianity and the Shona* (London: The Athlone Press, 1969), 49.

11 John S. Mbiti, *Concepts of God in Africa* (New York: Praeger Publication, 1970),218.

I also agree with Mbiti on the idea of one's relationship with God, others, and one's beliefs. Collective and communal beliefs have an impact on how one relates to or perceives God. The above statement, "he believes because others believe," may not be as simple as it reads. The statement, "one may believe because others believe," may mean that one knows that if what s/he believes along with the community is wrong, then s/he is not the sole person accountable for the wrong belief. Rather, the whole community is accountable.

Many creation stories and myths in the African context point to the importance of relationships between God, humanity, and creation in general. In the traditional Shona society, myths serve as the traditional interpretations of the universe and all of creation; they were used by the elders to explain the origin of things to the children. Many of the myths explained the Shona people's understanding of their relationships with God and creation. These myths are still significant in the traditional Shona society in so much as they help guide some of the people's behaviors in relating to God. The myths are still told today in more traditional contexts such as the rural areas. The purpose of using the myths in this book is to show how the traditional Shonas view their relationship with God from the time of creation. These myths were never adopted by the Shona Christian church due to their origins in the pagan world. In losing the African myths, the Shonas also lost grounding in their relational understanding of God, creation, and the Spirit World. The following section presents myths referring to the relationships between God and humanity.

One of the main problems is that the Shona Christian church does not adopt the Shona myths about relationships, since everything from African traditional religion was condemned as heathen. Banana, a Zimbabwean theologian, defines myth as both sacred history and reality, and sees a relationship between myths and theology:

> Myths explain origins of things. Theology is also concerned with the why, whence, of human and societal life, the basic conditions and goals of history, ultimate reality and ultimate concerns. Theology cannot be pursued simply within the framework of Western scientific language. . .The role of mythology gets particularly significant in African theology, where Christian articulation has to

> relate to traditional African concepts of life which are preserved and conveyed by means of mythology. [12]

The relationship between God, humans, and creation is explained in myths. In some creation myths, God was not just close to creation, but lived among the original people created. God used to dwell with humans, and everything was peaceful and God provided. The Shonas have a myth about how the separation between God and humanity took place. This myth is told by the Karanga who are also part of the Shona people in Zimbabwe:

> The close God is part of this creation as a father is part of his child. . .And the distant God? He came into existence when men disregarded his commandments. . . .When men no longer obeyed God, he retreated into the sky (or high mountain) and let men know "You did not obey me, I leave you. Your land will be dry and salt, thistles will grow on it, and there will be no rain. You will be killed by spears and will be slaves until you return to me." Thus evil came to the world. [13]

Separation from God was caused by humanity's disobedience. Humanity suffered and there was chaos among humans due to the separation. However, most myths conclude by saying that God never abandoned humanity, and/or God's relationship with humanity never ceased to exist.

To maintain the relationship between God and humanity, rituals and worship came into place. What Mbiti says about the way to maintain the relationships is also believed true in the traditional Shona society:

> And so the original direct contact and relationship between God and man was broken. The unfortunate consequences for man include the loss of immortality, resurrection, rejuvenation, and free food in addition to the coming of death and suffering. Yet, through acts of worship, man tries to counteract this separation and to maintain. . .contact with God.[14]

---

12 Canaan S. Banana, *Come and Share* (Gweru: Mambo Press, 1991), 34. For a more detailed discussion on what is myth, mythmaking in Africa, myth, and social reality, see Isidore Okpewho, *Myth in Africa: A Study of its Aesthetic and Cultural Relevance* (Cambridge: Cambridge University Press, 1982).

13 H. Aschwanden, *Karanga Mythology* (Gweru: Mambo Press, 1989), 216.

14 Mbiti, *Concepts of God in Africa*, 177.

Even though the separation referred to in the myth seems to put God very far away from humanity (One who is transcendent), God is perceived as very immanent in honoring the agreement between God and humanity to maintain the relationship, despite separation. The following myth is generally shared among Shona:

> Thus the Karanga [a Shona subgroup] speak of a God who is distant and close simultaneously. They say: "God is far away in the sky, but he is with us too (*Mwari ari kure kudenga kumusoro-soro asi ari pedo nesu*)." . . .Also everyday names convey the impression that God is near. When God is called grandmother *(ambuya)* or ancestor (*mudzimu*) he is honored by terms which are very meaningful to the Karanga and close to their heart. The reality of God manifests itself also in the defenseless, the orphans and the unborn, as well as the insane- all of whom can bear his name.[15]

The idea of God's transcendence is understood more in terms of God's limitlessness and boundlessness. In this sense the Shonas are saying that God fills and controls the universe and the whole of creation. Even the moon, sun, and stars are under God's control and order. Transcendence does not prevent God from being involved in the affairs of humanity or being in relationship with humanity. The Shonas understand God as immanent and closer to them than their breath. Most African prayers plead for God's protection, not as a remote God, but as a God who is close. God's protection is sought at night while one is sleeping and on long journeys. God is not far removed, but close enough that humanity can easily approach God in prayer or times of need.[16]

The continual relatedness of God to humanity, even after the separation of God and humanity, is also found in the attributes the Shona people associate with God. God is seen as Father, Mother, love, kindness, merciful, provider, just, good, faithful, holy, and righteous, etc. Humanity is also perceived as God's children and relates to God as in the context of family relationships. God is seen as *Mudzimu mukuru*, meaning the "Great Ancestor," or *Tateguru*, "Great Grandmother or the one who gave birth to

---

15 Aschwanden, Karanga Mythology, 210 & 211.

16 Mbiti, *Concepts of God in Africa*, 171.

all the people." As God's children, people can easily approach God through prayer and worship in times of need and crisis.

> A mother is to her children what God is to men. . .God is like an *(ambuya)*, it is said. He gives to all good and bad, and like an *ambuya* he welcomes everybody and is as generous as she is. One expression says: God's goodness and mercy are like an *ambuya* who is quick to forgive her grandchildren *(ngoni netsitsi dzaMwari dzakaita sambuya vasingatani kukanganwira vazukuru)*[17]

However, there are also attributes which point to God as a God of anger and a judge who can avenge. These attributes describe God in anthropomorphic terms, and, even more so, in terms of God's interpersonal relationship with humanity. In times of need, people turn to God because they believe God's nature to be loving, merciful, kind, and just. God's loving mercies and kindness are seen or understood in "concrete terms" of humanity's day-to-day survival. Practical experiences of how God provides food, shelter, rain, etc., are given as concrete examples of how God is in relationship with the Shona people.

Muzorewa echoes the fact that in addition to the communal aspect of salvation for the Africans (which includes the Shonas), salvation is also based upon tangible and visible acts of God, for and/or within the community.

> Africans believe that while God is invisible, God's acts are tangible. . .This is why African theology believes both that God is spirit and that God's presence can be felt and experienced physically. African theology needs to explicate the doctrine of the Holy Spirit in such a way that believers may feel the tangibleness of the benefits of knowing Christ.[18]

Good harvest, hunting, or fishing seasons are more signs of God's interpersonal involvement in humanity's affairs. God's love is experienced when God intervenes in times of calamities or natural disasters. The idea of God's love is also experienced in God's salvation.

God's salvation is also a communal experience. When God does not send rain, or sends an earthquake to a community because of the sin or act

17 H. Aschwanden, *Karanga Mythology*, 204.

18 Muzorewa, *The Origins and Developments*, 11-12.

of an individual, it affects the entire community. In the same vein, when God blesses or saves an individual, this salvation or blessing is for the benefit of the community as well. This is contrary to the personal responsibility taught and preached to the Shona by Western Christianity.

Maimela makes the argument, with which this writer totally concurs, that, "It will therefore not do to try to understand what sin and salvation are in African Traditional Religions from a purely Christian perspective in which salvation is usually understood to be an individualistic unburdening of personal sin through what happened to Jesus Christ on the cross."[19] At another, level sin and salvation affect the individual psychologically, physically, and spiritually inasmuch as the rituals involved require physical, mental, emotional, and spiritual engagement. Individual sin or salvation affect more than the individual; they also affect the community psychologically and spiritually.

Offending God causes chaos and disharmony. God is perceived as One who can become angry. When humanity commits moral transgressions such as murder, incest, etc., God's anger is stirred, thereby bringing disharmony to the community. The Shonas believe that disobedience, wickedness, and evil-heartedness anger God and cause chaos, bringing meaninglessness and disequilibrium to interpersonal relationships in the lives of the society or the community. There are rules and customs used for purposes of social and religious regulations. Breaking such rules and customs creates disharmony in the relationship between humanity and God. Murphree says about disobeying a custom such as the holy day of *chisi* (a day of rest), "Breaches of these regulations would be punished by Mwari sending. . . calamity to the person and property of the offenders."[20]

The relationship with God is both corporate and communal. The Shona understanding of God is realized through relationships with or being related to God. God is not One who is just experienced mentally, but is One who, through relationship to humanity, reveals God's Self. God is transcendent, but at the same time very close to humanity. God's relationship with humanity is not impersonal but is an interpersonal relational reality.

19 Maimela, "Salvation in African Traditional Religions," 66.

20 Murphree, *Christianity and the Shona*, 49-50.

Human Relationships. In the Shona society, that an individual's personal and religious identity is based on one's community of embeddedness is a matter that is viewed as a given. One acquires authenticity or individual identity based on his or her community of embeddedness or communal existence. If one destroys the individual, one destroys an entity of the community. At the same time, if one destroys the community, one destroys the individual or an essential part of the individual. This affects how issues of sin, forgiveness, and salvation are perceived in human relations among the Shonas.

Sin, in the Shona context, is defined in terms of relationships rather than in mental or philosophical ideas. Anything evil which one does to harm the other is sin. In any situation where right relationships are absent, sin has occurred. This is different from the Western Christian understanding of sin in terms of original sin. Sin is normally an act that one commits against the other, and one that brings about chaos among interpersonal relationships with the other. The "other" in the context of the human community may mean a relative or a stranger. Peaden notes:

> . . .adultery, theft, murder, and untruthfulness were wrong [the Shona believed] and had rules about the duty of helpfulness to members of their family. They also believed that a person had a duty to the stranger, to help him if he was passing through their village while on a journey. These morals did not arise from a belief about pleasing or displeasing Mwari, but rather from a conception of a just society and from the necessity of keeping harmonious personal relationships within a close-knit community.[21]

While for the traditional Shonas, acts of violence such as murder, incest, thievery, putting a curse on someone, or witchcraft are considered sin, even being inhospitable to a stranger is to be avoided, since this could cause disharmony with the stranger's community. Moyo, a Zimbabwean, suggests the following regarding sin and human relationships:

> Traditional societies understand sin as any action violating the integrity of God's creation, disrupting relationships within the family and community as a whole and bringing suffering or even death. A sinful action may deprive the individual and his or her community of peace, happiness, wellness and prosperity. Repentance

21 W. R. Peaden, *Missionary Attitude to the Shona Culture* (Salisbury [Harare]: The Central Africa Historical Association, 1970), 2.

> must therefore involve the whole community and not just the individual. . .In other words, one actually sins against God by sinning against one's neighbour. The emphasis is on relationships here and now, but those relationships ultimately affect one's relation to God and the living dead, who then cease to offer protection to the sinner and the members of his family. God and the ancestors can never be on the side of the sinner until the sinner comes to deal justly with others in the community.[22]

Christianity came to Africa preaching individual responsibility, sin, and salvation for one's actions. Contemporary Shona Christians will make statements such as, *Musha wekwa nhingi une ngozi*, which translates into "the village or family of so and so is being hounded by an avenging spirit." A similar saying *Ndezve dzinza, kana kuti ndezve chidzinza*, suggests that "someone or a family is being affected by an evil deed committed by someone in the previous generation or by previous generations." People do not place sole responsibility on the individual who committed the crime, rather blame is placed on the whole family or community.

In spite of their Christianity, those Christians whose families have relatives who have committed crimes of murder live in fear and anxiety because they believe that the avenging spirit can hound them. This belief calls for them to be involved in traditionally known rituals as a way to right their relationship with God, the deceased, and with the family/ community of the deceased. Christians, however, are forbidden by the church to participate in these traditional rituals. Western Christianity teaches that whoever committed the crime is the one who needs to be forgiven by God and reconciled to the person s/he sinned against. More specifically, Christianity's stance is that reconciliation is between the sinner and God, and sometimes the one sinned against. For those urban Shona Christians, who believe there is need for the rituals of accountability and reconciliation with the deceased and the deceased's family, this creates anxiety, because the ritual of exorcism sanctioned by the church for this process is only one part of the entire ritual.

Forgiveness, then, is not just for the individual but for the whole community. Rituals of forgiveness in the traditional society involve the entire community. A community's perceived guilt stems from the

---

22 Moyo, *Zimbabwe: The of Incarnation*, 40-41.

perception that they should have intervened on behalf of the guilty person before he /she committed the evil act. In some cases, forgiveness may end up involving more than the individual and the human community and may also include nature and the Spirit World. Moyo says about the act of incest in traditional Zimbabwean society, "It is so grave that it affects all of God's creation. Rains are withheld as punishment, leading to severe drought, with all the consequences this has for a people who depend on cattle and farming for livelihood."[23] Thus in the traditional society, the sin of incest committed by an individual can affect the entire community including creation.

Relationship Between Nature and Humanity. In the African world, one is raised with the consciousness that nature and all of creation are interdependent. I concur with Banana's notion that Africans understand God in "ontological terms," meaning there is no doubt in the minds or beliefs of the Africans that God's existence is a given and that, "Traditionally, Zimbabweans experience God's revelation also in natural phenomena such as trees, rocks, caves, rivers, and also mountains. . .in African traditional religions there were no atheists; all members of a particular society belonged to the religion of that society."[24] Creation reveals God's works and continuous creativity. All of creation exists for reciprocal benefit and is to be respected.

Among the Shonas, and most other African traditions and cultures, humanity is believed to have been created out of the soil. I remember, when still young, asking my late grandmother why there were different colors of people. My grandmother took me outside to different places in the yard and the field surrounding the home. My grandmother instructed me to touch and feel the different types and textures of the soil, and asked me to tell her what different colors the soils were. Some of the soil was red clay, black, greyish, brown etc. She related to me how the Shona people believe that humans were created from the soil and as soil has different color and texture so too do human beings differ in color. She went further to say that not only were we created out of the soil, but that the earth is our Mother,

---

23 Ibid, 40-41.

24 Banana, *Come and Share*, 40.

and that all of life comes out of, or is connected to, the earth. This story she instructed me to pass to my children.

The Shonas strongly believe that what hurts the earth hurts all of creation, including humanity. Anything which may upset the balance of nature (including trees, animals, etc.) will hurt humanity. The forces of nature such as earthquakes, drought, storms, etc. are real; however, nature is to be used for human survival but must be used with respect, not abused. The Western idea of humanity "dominating" the earth is foreign to the African context. We were created to be in relationship and harmony with the earth. There are traditional festivals and rituals held before ploughing or planting crops. The purpose of the ritual is at two levels: the first purpose is to ask God and the ancestors to bless the seeds and send the rains in time. Aschwanden, who researched among the Karanga (Shona subgroup) about their mythologies and wrote a book about the myths, says of the sowing ritual among the Shona:

> Before sowing starts, the chief collects seed of all sorts in a basket and takes it to the tribe's leading medium. He offers a handful of seed to the medium - palm up: he shows it to those in the "sky" and prays to the ancestors especially to the most important one of the tribe (*mudzimu mukuru,* also called *shumba yomudzimu)* as well as to God. The prayer says: "The time of sowing has arrived. We ask for your blessing for a good harvest. God, give us rain and keep the insects off the plants, also the grasshoppers. And you, ancestors, look after our fields so the sun does not shine on them too brightly." . . .The people then all return home with a handful of the blessed seed and mix it with their own seed. In this way a good crop is to be secured.[25]

A second purpose of the planting ritual is to announce to Mother Earth that humans are going to be cutting wounds into her and that no harm is intended. This is to make certain that all the relationships are right with God/ Spirit World, and with the land.

The important aspect of the rituals had to do with relationships to the Spirits of the area, as well as the maintenance of right relationships with "Mother Earth." Humans are taught to maintain good relationships with their environment and with nature and the Spirit world. Bourdilion notes about the need for maintenance of these relationships:

---

25 Aschwanden, *Karanga Mythology*, 225.

> Any projects of significance, such as building of dams or a school, should have the approval of the spirits of the area. These spirits are usually the ancestors of the chief who is their living representative: in such a case, they are approached through the chief who is their appointee. The chief is closely associated with the land precisely because as the senior descendant of the original owners. . .but this ownership is restricted to very limited rights over the land and certain duties towards it.[26]

The idea of owning land was also foreign to the Africans. No one had a "title deed" over a piece of land. Contrary to the Shona culture and tradition, the Westerners introduced the idea of land ownership. Peaden says, "On the other hand there were the hereditary Shona chiefs to whom the occupation of land was a sacred trust inherited from their forefathers and to whom the question of selling or otherwise permanently alienating land could not arise."[27] The Shona was to take care of the land; he or she ploughed it, and eventually it would be left to rejuvenate after a period of time. Land belonged to the Creator, not to humanity, and humanity is to live in interdependence with it.

I believe many Westerners misunderstood the fact that Africans can address a tree as if it had a soul, and the Westerners believed that action to be animism. However, for a traditional Shona, a spirit can be believed to be dwelling in a tree yet the spirit is not part of the make-up of the tree. As a person can live in a home and move on to another, leaving the first one vacant, it is in the same sense that a spirit can claim residence in a tree and be territorial but can also move on; it is not the make-up of the tree. If one destroys the dwelling place for a Spirit without a ritual, that is when misfortune may occur. In addition, there are certain trees considered sacred due to rituals performed by the community under those trees or just because the community deem the surrounding places and trees sacred. Again, the main purposes of the traditional Shona rituals are to maintain healthy interpersonal communal existence with that which surrounds humans.

---

26 Bourdillon, *The Shona Peoples*, 68 & 69.

27 Peaden, *Missionary Attitude to the Shona Culture*, 5.

The Shona Pastoral Caregiver and Prohibition of Traditional Religious Practices. The advent of Christianity meant the Shona had to shift from their involvement from Shona traditional religio-cultural communal activities to ones which were individualistic and ones which, in many ways, were contrary to those with which the Shona were familiar. A shift from the traditional Shona understanding of relationships to a Western Christian understanding was forced upon those Shonas who converted to Christianity.

The prohibition by the Shona Christian church of the utilization of some aspects of traditional religious practices and rituals by pastoral caregivers proves to be a handicap. In order for relational pastoral theology of care to be relevant in addressing the contemporary urban Shona pastoral care needs, the pastoral caregiver must be familiar with the suppressed history of Shona traditional relational theology. As aforementioned, relational theology is a theology whose primary focus is on the dynamics and understanding of relationships between humans, humanity and God, God humanity, and nature or creation.[28] The community relations extend beyond the human community to include God, the Spirit World, and all of creation. This would allow the caregiver to understand the struggles of the urban Shona Christians.

Even though there was a shift in religious doctrine and ideology, the urban Shona Christians are still aware of the traditional beliefs of being responsible for a family member's actions. The ceremonies and rituals such as *chenura* (cleansing ritual), *kupira mudzimu* (veneration of ancestors), consultation of the *n'anga* (medicine person) and polygamy, used in this chapter, illustrate issues of interpersonal relationships lost through the advent of Christianity. The prohibition of these ceremonies and rituals impacts both the urban and rural Shona Christians. In the urban context, however, the impact is readily recognizable in that for most Shona Christians the church provides them with a primary sense of a community of embeddedness, as opposed to the rural context in which the village community along with the church gives the sense of embeddedness.

---

28 Colin A. Russell, *The Earth, Humanity and God* (London: UCL Press, 1994).

Moyo notes about the experience of the Zimbabwean Christians today:

> While many Christians today manifest respect for the departed ancestors and take part in ceremonies relating to them, openly, many others do so only privately. They live a Christian life during the day and live the real African life during the night, resulting in what Desmond Tutu and others have described as a kind of schizophrenia. . .[29]

Some Shona Christians may not fully trust the solutions prescribed by Christianity; hence, they become anxious and feel guilty when they try to solve the problems by utilizing traditional methods condemned by Western Christianity. My argument is that the Shona Christian church needs to revisit its rules and rituals as pertaining to integration of some traditional practices which are not necessarily contrary to Christian teachings, so as to give both the Shona Christian and the pastoral caregiver more freedom in how they practice Christianity in this context.

Illustrative of the dilemma experienced by Shona Christians is when they visit the medicine person by night, with the hope that no other Christians see them, to address a crisis the family may believe needs the African traditional solution and for which Christian rituals may seem inadequate. If the behavior of these Christians (visiting the medicine person) is discovered, it creates anxiety in them since they have engaged in something which is contrary to Christian beliefs.

Despite the time which has passed, and even with the present United Methodist indigenous-led church in Zimbabwe, the Shona United Methodists still follow most of the beliefs established by the early missionaries. This has perpetuated the problem of bi-religiousness and results in creating anxiety as some of these Christians try to pay respect to their traditional religion, which in the eyes of the church is in conflict with true Western Christianity.

Anxiety arises as a result of Shona Christians mixing the traditional beliefs, not sanctioned by the church, with the ones prescribed by the church. This writer also agrees with Kapenzi, believing that one of the major sources of the bi-religiousness and bi-culturalism in the contemporary Shona context results from the church's failure to revisit

29 Moyo, *Zimbabwe: The Risk of Incarnation*, 19-20.

traditional practices condemned by Western Christianity, yet deemed necessary to the faith of the Shona Christian today. Kapenzi summarizes this well:

> For conversion to the Christian faith to be more than superficial, the Christian church must come to grips with traditional beliefs and practices and with the world view that these beliefs and practices imply. It would be unreal not to recognize the fact that many church members are influenced in their conduct by traditional beliefs and practices and by the traditional interpretation of the universe. The new convert is poised between two worlds: the old traditions and customs of his culture which he is striving to leave behind, and the new beliefs and practices to which he is still a stranger.[30]

The church today is similarly not preserving or integrating some of the traditional rituals, even those not contrary to the Christian teachings. Mental, psychological, and religious conflict occurs when a Shona Christian tries to live a Christian life and at the same time engages in some of the Shona traditional religious practices which involve relationships with the family or community. Does one supplant one's relationships with the family one loves in order to respect one's religious beliefs? Christians are forbidden to engage in such rituals as *chenura* (a cleansing or purification ritual); this is a peace and justice-making ritual, performed by the family for the dead person. Since everything from traditional Shona religion was considered heathen or pagan, it was banned with the advent of the Christian church. In the traditional Shona theological world-view, a dead person is still believed to be part of, and in relationship with, the community. Tension, guilt, and anxiety befalls people in situations where Shona Christians try to engage in traditional rituals or ignore such sayings as, *MaKristo haiti zvinhu zwechivanhu* (Christians are not to involve themselves in Shona traditional religious ways). However, the traditional Shonas, and some of the contemporary urban people, believe that one must always honor and respect one's elders or ancestors. Since life continues after death, honor, respect, and one's relationship with the deceased (ancestors) are not concluded by the burial ceremony.

---

30 Geoffrey Z. Kapenzi, *The Clash of Cultures: Christian Missionaries and the Shona of Rhodesia [Zimbabwe]* (Washington, D.C.: University Press of America, 1979), 35.

Conflict arises within families as some members adhere to the Shona traditional practices while others try to adhere to the Christianity prescribed by the church. Furthermore, others in the same family might be comfortable with mixing the two religious practices and beliefs. Peaden notes:

> Christians also came under heavy pressure by non-Christian relatives to conform to traditional patterns, especially in times of trouble and sickness. . .It is more often recorded that Christians in time of trouble themselves consulted *nganga*. They could scarcely do this unless they believed that the cause of the trouble lay with the spirit of their ancestors, or that the trouble would end if the proper ceremonies were carried out.[31]

Tension results because bi-religiousness within family systems is common among the Shonas today. For some, the conflict is within themselves, not knowing which beliefs to follow. In situations where, due to the lack of substitute Christian rituals, the Shona is forced to choose involvement in or performance of the traditional religio-cultural rituals which have been condemned as heathen, anxiety is the result.

The ritual to resolve a situation of a *ngozi* (avenging spirit) is another example of how one can be caught between religions in the attempt to resolve interpersonal relational problems. The ritual to resolve the problem of a *ngozi* was never adopted by the church because it had its roots in the African traditional religion and culture. In the United Methodist hymnal there is a song, *Nengozi dzingapere dzose pamuchinjikwa,* which translates to, "the avenging spirits are destroyed at the cross." By singing this song, the Shona Christians are claiming their belief in the existence and powers of the *ngozi* spirit. However, the church did not accept the traditional ritual to solve interpersonal relations of this kind, since the ritual is from the Shona traditional religion. Western Christianity stated that the only religious requirement for the person who committed an act of murder was to believe in and to be forgiven by Christ, and to have an exorcism of the avenging spirit performed.

The avenging spirit (the deceased victim) hounds the family because it seeks the reasons why it was murdered, an accountability for the murder, acts of restitution, and the recreation of harmony within the families

31 Ibid., 34-35.

involved. The deceased's family seeks justice for the murder of its relative, but there is no Christian ritual for this to occur. The traditional ritual to resolve the problem of *ngozi* is, in my perspective, a theologically sound ritual which addresses the issues of interpersonal relationships between humans, God, and the Spirit World.[32]

Because traditional rituals are prohibited by the church, again, tension arises in some families or individuals regarding the ritual of *chenura* (cleansing ritual). The church has not done much to change or to integrate some of the aspects of this ritual from the traditional religion which may not necessarily be contrary to Christianity. The *chenura* ritual is a reconciling ritual between the living and the deceased which is performed sometime after burial. This is a ritual at which the spirit of the deceased is sent off to join the spirit world.

Yet another example of interpersonal relationships creating anxiety in mainline churches is polygamy. Christianity banned polygamy for all who converted, although it is not contrary to the Bible, especially the Old Testament. In the United Methodist church, and other mainline denominations, those polygamous men who convert to and who want to participate fully as members are forced to divorce all their wives except the first one.[33] Western Christianity demands that, in order to qualify as a true Christian, a man abandon secondary and subsequent wives and their children, whom he loves, and remain only with the first wife and her children. A polygamous man cannot be a true Christian and therefore cannot receive baptism or be accorded a full Christian burial ritual. Muzorewa also writes on this issue and notes that polygamy is not contradictory to the Christian teaching based on the Old Testament. Instead, Western ideals defined polygamy as a moral wrong. It was a

---

32 Tapiwa N. Mucherera, *Pastoral Care and Counseling in the Shona Context: Reclaiming Shona Traditional Healing Methods* (MA Thesis) (Denver Colorado: Taylor Library, 1994). In this thesis, the author uses mostly inculturation theological material. In this book this writer does not directly utilize the inculturation material, but makes reference to it by the way of the M.A. thesis.

33 Ronald P. Patterson, ed., *The Book of Discipline of the United Methodist Church: Africa Central Conference Edition* (Nashville: The United Methodist Publishing House, 1990), 53.

practice in which Westerners did not believe; hence, the missionaries condemned it.[34]

When misfortune, calamities, or illness repeatedly strike a family or a community in the Shona traditional community, it is usually concluded that aspects of interpersonal relationships are out of balance. The logical traditional solution is to go to the medicine person (*N'ganga*) or the seer (*mushoperi*) to get information about the source of the problem *(kooshopera)*. The seer advises the family or community regarding the causes of illnesses or calamities and about the possible rituals to be performed in order to solve the problem. Moyo notes about the struggles of the Shona Christians in addressing such situations:

> It is common among Zimbabwean Christians of all denominations, including pastors, to participate, in times of prolonged illness or other misfortunes in the family, in the traditional rituals relating to the departed elders. Some Christians stop going to church or away from the Lord's Supper or active participation in church life for a while in order to give themselves time to perform the traditional rites and make the required sacrifices to bring about healing in the family. When they have completed what the traditional diviners have prescribed in relation to the departed elders and spirits, they return to the church authorities to request absolution. African pastors who are close to their people know that these things are happening in both the rural and urban settings.[35]

Anything involving an African medicine person was perceived by the missionary as evil since the medicine person was believed to be using "powers of darkness." This remains the church's stance today, so one cannot consult the seer or medicine person.

As much as most Shona Christians believe in modern medicine, there are some diseases still believed to be curable only by the medicine person. Illnesses referred to as *zwechivanhu,* (diseases only curable using traditional medicine) cause considerable psychological conflict for the Shona Christians. Peaden gives an example of such a situation:

> European medicines, although in many ways superior to the drugs that the *nganga* gave, were not infallible and there were many illnesses which they were not able to cure. On the other hand the *nganga* were able to cure some that the Europeans

---

34 Muzorewa, *The Origins and Developments*, 31-32.

35 Moyo, *Zimbabwe: The Risk of Incarnation*, 20.

> could not. . .On one occasion, for example, an African teacher was admitted to hospital for observation after suffering for several weeks. . .After a week the European doctor told the writer that nothing physically wrong could be found with the teacher who was then discharged. He thereupon went to an *nganga* and after doing what the *nganga* prescribed, the pain disappeared; and a year later there had been no recurrence of the pain. . .the Shona distinguish between the physical working of an illness and its spiritual cause.[36]

Those Shona Christians who might perceive it necessary to go to a medicine person or seer for the solution to their problems do not have such freedom or permission from the church. Engaging in such behavior is an "evil" which could warrant one's placement on probationary membership in the church (United Methodist) and sometimes results in excommunication from the Holy Communion table. Peaden says, "Many of the rules conflicted with the Shona traditions, and those who broke them were censured by their church. There was a tendency for churches to administer discipline in a rigid and legalistic way, to the exclusion of charity and forgiveness."[37] Some of the same legalistic and rigid tendencies referred to by Peaden, and established by the missionaries, are still part of the Shona Christian churches today.

An Alternative Approach for Shona Pastoral caregiver. One of the main reasons Christianity fails to meet the emotional and spiritual needs of the Shona is the removal of some of the rituals ingrained psychologically in the minds of the Shona; they were thrown out by the church when they were deemed heathen. In this book I am not arguing that the church must embrace everything from the Shona traditional religion. However, if the church is going to train pastors to have an integrative consciousness, it must train Shona pastors with a relevant relational pastoral theology, that is: (a) a pastoral theology conversant with both world-views, with African pastoral theology as a starting point; and (b) a pastoral theology which re-evaluates the relationship between Christian rituals and the Shona traditional rituals, creating integrated rituals.

---

36 Peaden, *Missionary Attitude to the Shona Culture*,18.

37 Ibid., 4 & 5.

In training of the Shona pastoral caregivers, I concur with the pastoral theological approach used by Wimberly and Smith in pastoral theology of care.[38] Both Wimberly and Smith advocate for a pastoral theological approach which gives priority to people's narratives and stories when one tries to understand their theological view point. One of the reasons is that story telling in sharing one's struggles and hurts is very common and comes very natural to most Shona people. I believe that, out of the narratives presented to the pastoral theologian and/or caregiver, the caregiver can then identify the problems in faulty interpersonal relationships. These narratives provide the pastoral caregiver with images and a sense of the individual's or individuals' discernment through elucidating interpersonal relationships in which God or others are or are not at work in their lives. Out of the narration of the stories, the faulty interpersonal relationships are presented, revealing the points at which the anxiety arises, causing the care receiver to seek help from the pastoral caregiver.

To illustrate the use of narrative in the Shona context, I will relate another incident that happened with my grandmother. When I was between the ages of five and eight years old, I struggled with low self-esteem. I was very small in stature and it seemed everyone could easily bully me. I started school at six years of age and was not doing well. One day as I sat with my grandmother I questioned her about my little cousin's hands.[39] I had noticed that when my cousin came home from the hospital after birth her hands were clasped into a fist, and after about three or so weeks the hands had started unfolding. I asked my grandmother why it was that when my cousin was born the hands were folded into a fist, and now they were unfolded. My grandmother again narrated that, we the Shona people believe that when infants are born they have their hands clamped into a fist because they are holding all the gifts, graces, talents, and uniqueness given to them by God at their creation. After a few weeks their hands start to unfold. This is a sign to the world that they are willing to share with the world the gifts

---

38 Edward P. Wimberly, *Recalling Our Own Stories: Spiritual Renewal for Religious Care-givers* (St. Francisco, Jossy-Bass, 1997); Archie Smith, *Navigating the Deep River: Spirituality in African-American Families* (Ohio: United Church Press, 1997).

39 I shared this story as a devotional in *The Upper Room*, Oct 11, 1994, p. 46.

and graces God gave them. She went on to say that this was the same way I came into the world. She said she had noticed and heard me talk negatively about myself and how I felt I could never amount to much. God did not create me for rubbish nor failure, she said. There was something that God gave me at the time I was created that no one else in this world possessed. That which God had given me, no one else could give to the world as I could. She instructed me that every time I look at my hands to remember the story of a baby's hands and that I am unique. She went further to tell me that I was better in many ways at some things than the Europeans who were oppressing us and telling us that we Africans were backward and behaved as animals. God had created me a human being and I was not any less than anyone else. You can imagine what this narrative counseling session did to my self-esteem, my relationship with God, and others.

In addition, asking the following theological questions will help in the theological assessment of the careseeker's relationship with God and others. What is the careseeker's relationship with God and others? Based on the careseeker's communal interpersonal relations, what is the fundamental human predicament in terms of sin, salvation, and forgiveness? What ecologies of culture, nature, and interpersonal relationships are evident? What multiple communities are operative for good or ill? Based on the interpersonal relations narratives presented by the careseeker, what are the theological and spiritual outlooks? Are the spiritual and theological outlooks conflictual, inconsistent, or integrated? What is the meaning and quality of community for the careseeker? Where are the issues of brokenness, estrangement, abuse, forgiveness, justice, and reconciliation? What is the careseeker's source of hopelessness, anxiety and apathy, and how are these aspects connected to his or her communal interpersonal relations?[40] I am arguing that what brings people to the pastoral caregiver in the urban Shona context is anxiety, as a result of broken communal interpersonal relationships.

One of the main reasons for understanding traditional Shona relational theology is to note its continuing impact on the lives of contemporary urban

---

40 Graham, *Care of Persons, Care of Worlds.*

Shona Christians. I am challenging the church to re-evaluate the rituals, theology, and practice of ministry in order to assure their relevance to the contemporary Shona Christian. In order to equip Shona pastors with a relevant pastoral theology of care, pastors are to be trained with a consciousness which is conversant with both world-views, to facilitate integration of traditional Shonas with the Western world-view. The next chapter presents case studies and analysis to illustrate this need.

CHAPTER FIVE

Case Studies, Analysis, and Suggested Pastoral Responses

Kare hagari ari kare, which translates as, "The past will not remain the past," meaning, "Change is inevitable," is a Shona saying which influences the ways in which the traditional Shona people perceive life; it addresses life's changes, an issue which permeates the Shona understanding of life and influences the ways in which the Shonas live. Their religious and theological understanding about life's changes reflects this philosophy. However, the type of change brought about by Western Christianity, colonization, and urbanization created alienation and anxiety in the contemporary urban Shona Christians. One reason for this conflict is attributable to the fact that the change was not generated from within, but rather came from outside the religion and culture. The change brought degradation, shame, dehumanization, oppression, and mental colonization. In short, the change was forced on the Shonas in a manner that was violent and imperialistic in nature. This change resulted in the psychological internalization of self degradation and the religious and cultural misconception by many Shonas that Western culture and Christianity were better than the alleged "paganistic" and "backward" traditional Shona religion and culture.

What is needed in the contemporary urban Shona context is positive change which addresses the anxiety produced by bi-culturalism and bi-religiousness, both of which resulted from colonization and Western Christianity. In doing the case analyses, this chapter suggests the types of change needed in the pastoral caregiver's training, to facilitate adequately addressing approaches to pastoral care in the urban contemporary Shona context. The following points raised by Maimela make a good introduction to the problems and case analyses:

> For while most African Christians have accepted the Christianity that has been taught to them by the missionaries, and find it attractive in many ways, they are puzzled by the fact that in the historic churches the reality of witchcraft is explicitly denied despite any experience of it. . .they are prohibited to consult with diviners and medicine men and women, and that the existence of spirits, especially ancestral spirits, are called into question. The consequence is that a large number of African Christians believe that the church is not interested in their daily misfortunes, illness, encounters with evil and witchcraft, bad luck, poverty, barrenness, - in short, all their concrete social problems. . .As to be expected, most Africans often do not know what to do with their new, attractive Christian religion and yet one which dismally fails to meet their emotional and spiritual needs [sic].[1]

The point Maimela is raising about Western Christianity's failure to meet the spiritual and emotional needs of most African Christians is one this author is raising as well. Rituals integrating the traditional Shona rituals with Western Christian rituals would better serve the urban Shona Christians. Maimela further notes:

> The reluctance of Africans to break ties with the African Traditional Religions lies in the fact that they are wedded to an African world-view in which salvation is understood in terms of relief or help in terms of trouble in this life. Salvation is thus expressed in such acts as healing, driving away evil spirits, empowerment of the individual self, the promotion of fertility, success in life ventures. . . [2]

The church must find ways to better meet the psychological and spiritual needs of the urban Shona Christians by raising questions about relevant ways in which to incorporate some traditional rituals into the life of the church rather than condemning these traditional rituals. One of my basic assumptions, as has been argued throughout this book, is that pastoral care

---

1 S. S. Maimela, "Salvation in African Traditional Religions," *Missionalia* 13 (Aug 1985), 71.

2 Ibid., 72.

approaches and methods need to be relevant, and therefore need to incorporate and integrate material from the traditional Shona religio-culture in serving the urban contemporary Shona Christians. Thus, the purpose of the following analysis is to highlight dilemmas experienced by these urban Shona pastoral caregivers who solely rely on Western rituals. Ultimately the rituals of the Western Christianity are inadequate. They do not provide effective comprehensive pastoral care since their fragmented approach fails to integrate rituals appropriate to traditional Shona religious culture, but heretofore condemned by Western Christianity.

Method of Analysis

Now, attention turns to a brief presentation of the method of analysis followed by a case-by-case analysis. These cited cases are representative of tensions within families in the urban context, as well as an embodiment of the tension experienced generally within the changing culture and religion of the urban Shona Christians. I am proposing that, for those providing pastoral care in the urban Shona context, the exploration of the following issues in pastoral care are essential: a socio-cultural analysis of the individual(s) involved in each of the cases, identifying anxiety and its sources including the psychological issues, and the religious and theological issues raised by the careseeker's narrative. I will first describe the aforementioned essential categories of case analysis, and then explore why it is relevant to use this approach. These categories were chosen simply because they aid the pastoral caregiver in the exploration of issues to be attuned to, in the struggles of bi-culturalism, bi-religiousness and anxiety connected to dysfunctional relationships with which the careseeker might be faced.

Socio-cultural Analysis

The socio-cultural analysis helps the pastoral caregiver understand the careseeker's culture of embeddedness. Understanding the careseeker's culture of groundedness helps the pastoral caregiver become attuned to cultural issues with which the careseeker might be struggling in a crisis.

When the pastoral caregiver is informed about the socio-cultural context of the careseeker, this knowledge aids the caregiver in determining an appropriate pastoral response, whether Western individualistic or communal in nature or both.

Due to the economic pressures in the urban areas, there is a tendency for the urban Shona to ignore the traditional communal and extended family-oriented lifestyle, and assimilate the Western individualistic nuclear family lifestyle instead. The socio-cultural analysis also helps the pastoral caregiver understand the extent to which the careseeker has assimilated Western cultural values. Anxiety can occur when these families try to turn to the extended family for help, and are rejected because they placed no value in their extended family interpersonal relationships before the crisis.

The socio-cultural analysis also provides the pastoral caregiver with information about the social or cultural upbringing of the careseeker. Since the traditional Shona religion and culture are closely intertwined, some of the traditional Shona cultural beliefs directly influence some of the religious beliefs. The pastoral caregiver providing care to the urban Shona Christian must be aware of these influences in order to address theologically issues which careseekers face. The knowledge of the careseeker's cultural world-view helps the pastoral caregiver understand the perspective (Western or Shona) in addressing the cultural issues raised by the careseeker.

Anxiety, its Sources, and Psychological Issues. Sullivan argues that the success of a therapist lies in his or her ability to recognize anxiety and the source of that anxiety in those seeking help. Based on Sullivan's premises, I argue that the pastoral caregiver must similarly be able to recognize the careseeker's source of anxiety. The main source of anxiety discussed in this book, in the urban Shona context, may not be depression or mental illness, and so forth, but rather is the result of bi-culturalism and bi-religiousness caused by the impact of the Western culture and Western Christianity on the urban Shona Christians.

For children growing up in such an environment, a lack of a sense of connectedness and communal interrelatedness results in developmental anxiety. The children growing up in the urban Shona context internalize the economic values of competition more than kinship or corporation. They grow up missing the value of traditional extended family relations. Crises arise when the children realize their lack of communal relations; confusion arises from being caught in a context of bi-culturalism and the subsequent absence of a particular culture with which to identify. The end result is a psychological and cultural dissonance.

Religious or Theological Issues. Due to the bi-religious experiences of the urban Shona Christians, there is a need to assess the careseeker's religious world-view. Inasmuch as the traditional Shona religion has been labeled heathen and paganistic, urban Shona Christians experience anxiety when attempting to utilize their traditional religion. It is from the careseeker's narrative that the pastoral caregiver can assess the theological themes and issues with which the careseeker is struggling. Paying attention to the individual narrative, in light of communal relations between the individuals involved, the careseekers' relationships with God and the Spirit World, along with their relations with other people and with all of creation, provides the caregiver with themes upon which to focus.

Suggested Pastoral Response. The goal in the pastoral caregiver's response is to suggest some of the traditional Shona rituals that could be integrated with Western Christian rituals. The idea is not to replace totally these Western Christian rituals; rather the objective is to add aspects from the traditional Shona religio-culture that may help address spiritual and psychological aspects now missing in the current rituals. The integration supplants the implicit criteria used by Western Christianity, which promoted the notion that anything from traditional Shona religio-culture is pagan. ma Mpolo argues that in providing pastoral care to the African Christian today, the pastoral caregiver must be ready to explore the how and why issues of illness, death, misfortunes, and so forth, including determining which ritual is needed to address each of these situations.[3] Most of the Shona Christian rituals adopted from Western Christianity do not answer these questions. On the other hand, traditional Shona rituals (not

3 ma Mpolo and Kalu, *The Risk of Growth*, 5ff.

contrary to Western Christianity) do help answer these questions raised by the careseekers.

A specific example is that of the ritual to resolve the problem of a *ngozi* spirit. The Western Christian ritual does not address the "how, why, and what" questions. The prescribed Shona Christian ritual adopted from Western Christianity is to exorcize the *ngozi* spirit, since the ngozi's actions of avenging itself are considered unchristian and evil. Exorcizing the *ngozi* does not give psychological and spiritual comfort to the Shona Christian, since s/he knows the *ngozi* spirit can move from one family member to another. In addition, the Shona Christian is aware that the processes to bring about justice, forgiveness, and reconciliation with the victim (*ngozi spirit*) and his/her family have not been followed. The traditional aspects of the ritual to resolve a *ngozi* situation preceding the exorcism itself answer the "how, why, and what" questions, in that the ritual involves accountability, restitution, and reconciliation processes for the two families.

As a discipline, pastoral care advocates for such processes of accountability, restitution, and reconciliation in situations which involve injustice and victimization.[4] This process is in agreement with the traditional Shona understanding in the *ngozi* spirit, since the *ngozi* spirit is a spirit of an individual trying to seek justice for an injustice done to him/her. Exorcizing the *ngozi* spirit without the accountability, restitution, and reconciliation ritual is victimizing the victim, which is what the current Shona Christian ritual does; it fails to address the whole problem and jumps to the end process of exorcism as found in traditional Shona religion.

The processes of accountability, restitution, and reconciliation are seen in the Christian teachings exemplified in the story of Zachaeus the tax collector. Jesus ordered him to go face his victims and repay what he owed them before reconciliation could take place. (Luke19:1-10).[5] In most (if not all) of the traditional Shona rituals used to address an injustice or to right people's dysfunctional interpersonal relationships in traditional Shona

---

4 Marie Fortune, *Is Nothing Sacred?* (San Francisco, Harper and Row, 1989).

5 Luke 19:1-10 *NRSV* (New Revised Standard Version).

society, the processes advocated as a criteria (accountability, restitution, and reconciliation) are involved; this would include addressing most death situations, illness, misfortunes, and catastrophes. Most of the Shona Christian rituals subvert the means to justice and forgiveness; rather, they advocate for forgiveness without the fully restorative process. I am suggesting incorporating some aspects of rituals from the traditional Shona religion to strengthen the Western Christian rituals in place and thus to be able to provide comprehensive psychological and spiritual peace for the Shona Christian. The following case studies and their analysis will help enlighten the reader with the argument proposed in this book.

Western Christianity Versus Shona Traditional Beliefs. *Mr. and Mrs. Dzobo, a Shona couple, live in a large four bedroom suburban home in Harare with their only son Robert. There is a rumor that there is a ngozi spirit hounding the family, because Mr. Dzobo's deceased parents killed someone for "muti" or medicine, in order for their business to prosper. Mr. Dzobo's parents died before anything was done to address the situation, and the Dzobos inherited the business from the parents, who both died in a car accident. The father died at the age of 49 and the mother was 47 years old. The same year Mr. Dzobo's parents died is the year Robert, the Dzobo's now 20 year-old only son, was born. Mr. Dzobo was 28 years of age when his parents died. It is said that Mr. Dzobo's uncle (the deceased father's only brother) did not attend the funeral. The uncle is reported to have said that he did not want to attend a funeral of or be associated with someone who had killed for financial gains. Thus, Mr. Dzobo buried his parents without much help from his extended family. Mr. Dzobo's relationship with his extended family is strained and no one has made an effort from either side to work things out.*

It is also said that the "ngozi" (the avenging spirit, or the spirit of the person reported as killed for use as "muti" for the business) had also manifested itself through a dream to Mr. Dzobo's father just before he died in the car accident. The avenging spirit is said to have told the deceased that he, his wife, and son would not live past 50 years of age. In the dream the ngozi also indicated that unless accountability, restitution, and justice took place the grandchild (Robert) would become a "rombe," which means

Robert would roam the streets, and sometimes exhibit signs of mental illness. The deceased parents had shared the dream with Mr. Dzobo and his wife.

Mr. and Mrs. Dzobo are members of the United Methodist church. Mrs. Dzobo has been accused of being proud and disrespectful by her in-laws and no one of the extended family wants to have much association with her. She prides herself as "a warrior in Christ," and says that "nothing will harm her family no matter what." Mrs. Dzobo says that anything evil that happens in her nuclear family is just "a test of her faith." She has openly verbally attacked those who have alluded to her family as one being hounded by an avenging spirit. Her family, she declares, "is covered by the blood of Christ, and no powers of darkness can overcome her family." She has called people from both sides of the extended families "heathens and pagans," and those whose minds are run and have been ruined by the devil. People say she also has a sharp tongue and that the husband is under a "petticoat government."

Robert, their son, sometimes acts as if he is mentally ill, but doctors have not been able to diagnose him. He calls himself "Tupac incarnate," abuses marijuana and alcohol, and mostly uses English to communicate. He has beaten the father twice to the extent that the father had to go to the hospital. He has confronted his parents about the issues of ngozi, and wants them to address this before they die (they are both close to 50 years of age). He says he is not vested in the Shona culture himself and would not know what to do if they die without reconciling with the ngozi. Robert has accused his parents of not being true Christians. How could true Christians inherit riches tainted with blood? If they were true Christians why do they not even speak to their close relatives? What type of God or Jesus do they believe in who allows them to hold grudges for life? One day, Robert locked himself in his room and talked in the third person, saying something had to be done to make things right. The Dzobos invited friends from church to help, to no avail, and now have turned to their pastor for help.

Socio-cultural Issues. The Dzobos are an economically prosperous family. They live as a nuclear family in a suburban home, with their only son, Robert. Their interpersonal relationships with their extended family are very poor. The Dzobos appear to live a family life which depends on the Western cultural values based on economic success rather than relying on their extended family relations. Even though they have not put it into words, the Dzobos appear to have come to the realization that economic success does not equal healthy interpersonal relations.

The Dzobos are caught between a Western culture, which emphasizes individual success based on material possessions and competition, and the traditional Shona culture, which gives priority to one's communal interpersonal relations and cooperation. The Dzobos acknowledge the centrality of communal interpersonal and extended family relations, but choose not to give priority to those relationships. In addition, their friends from church have not provided them with the cultural support system the Dzobos need inasmuch as these church friends also focus personal energy on their own economic success.

The Dzobos are caught between cultures, appear to have lost much of their Shona cultural heritage, and have apparently isolated themselves from participating in the Shona traditional religio-culture. The extended family appears to have also lost respect for Mr. Dzobo, whom they perceive to be "under a petticoat government." The lack of a clear culture of identity on the part of the parents has also affected Robert.

Robert has been left with no culture in which to feel "at home." Culturally, Robert is a "half-breed"; he does not have a specific cultural foundation. He has openly told his parents that he does not know much about the Shona culture. Robert grew up isolated from those places in which he could have learned some traditional culture. He does not know how to speak the Shona language well, nor does he understand the traditional culture issues of respect as pertaining to one's elders' expectations. On the other hand, the problem may be due to Robert's lack of awareness of the culture, indicating this conflict may need to be resolved through pastoral care which focuses on his relationship with his father.

Robert has immersed himself in the Western "rap" culture to the extent of calling himself "Tupac incarnate." On the other hand, Robert is instigating issues addressing the importance of communal interpersonal relations for the family. He complained that his family isolated him from his extended family while he was growing up, cutting him off from developing healthy communal relationships with the extended family. Exploring how economic (socio-cultural) realities play a part in placing them in the position in which they find themselves may help the Dzobos become less defensive (psychologically) and more willing to explore the realities of the problems they face.

Anxiety, its Sources, and Psychological Issues. There are at least two identifiable sources of the Dzobo family's anxiety on which the pastoral caregiver could focus, as a starting point. First, they do not have a communal support system since they have severed their relationships with their extended family. Their support system from church is more akin to that of business people who invest most of their time in economic success, and who have a lifestyle similar to that of the Dzobos.

Second, the Dzobos are experiencing religious anxiety by trying to reconcile the early deaths of Mr. Dzobo's parents (before the age fifty) and the behavior of Robert (already as announced by the *ngozi* spirit in the dream) with their Christian religious beliefs. They have publicly denounced the power of the *ngozi* spirit (a Shona traditional belief) but resolving their problems appears to indicate a need for integrating some traditional Shona religious beliefs as well. Choosing the Shona traditional ways with which to address the situation will mean going against their Christian belief systems. This has created religious dissonance for the Dzobos.

Robert is experiencing an individual identity crisis, based on a lack of a culture of embeddedness. He does not know who he is, Shona or Western? He has assimilated many Western values. However, he has come to believe in the powers of *ngozi* through the little knowledge he gained from studying the Shona traditional religion at the university. The parents have not helped decrease Robert's anxiety because they do not want to explore traditional religious remedies as a possible solution to the problem. Robert is anxiously struggling with the fact that his parents are now approaching the age of fifty (the deadline given by the *ngozi* as their life span). If nothing is done, and if the parents cannot take care of the *ngozi* situation and subsequently happen to die, Robert is left without a support system, since the parents cut him off from extended family relations. One way Robert has been coping with his anxiety is by abusing drugs and alcohol. Robert is an embodiment of the anxiety experienced by most of the culturally under-socialized children of the Shona urban context. He feels isolated and lost, and thus is experiencing psychological trauma.

Mr. and Mrs. Dzobo are dealing with their anxiety by denying the power of the *ngozi* spirit. Mrs. Dzobo uses her religious beliefs as a way to defend herself against those who allude to the avenging spirit. She appears to have "blind faith," faith which does not allow the voice of reason to help solve problems. In addition, both parents appear to be experiencing cultural dissonance. They have not put much effort into creating healthy interpersonal relationships with the extended family. They view the extended family members as "heathens and pagans" with whom they do not wish to associate.

Robert's mental state, and the fact that the Dzobos are both close to fifty years of age, may be forcing them to reconsider their situation, which has placed them in a state of anxiety. Their experience of broken communal interpersonal relations is also resulting in anxiety.

Theological or Religious Issues. The Dzobos' interpersonal relationships comprise the main theological or religious issues which the pastoral caregiver would find worthy of pursuit. The Dzobos' interpersonal relations are not only a concern as they pertain to other family members, but are also impaired in connection with God and the Spirit World. Based on a Shona relational pastoral theology, the examination of their relationship with others, God, Spirit World, and creation will aid in bringing to the surface most of the issues they need to address. They face the challenge of having to answer Robert's question: how can they call themselves true Christians while holding lifelong grudges against other extended family members? Mr. and Mrs. Dzobo refuse to face the issue of their interpersonal relations by projection - they ignore facing the problem raised by Robert, and focus instead on Robert's drinking problems. From both religious perspectives, the Dzobos need to consider re-establishing many communal interpersonal relationships in order to make things right.

Their own immediate family must face interpersonal relations issues. Even though the father may not believe in the traditional view that Robert's beating him is a traditional religio-cultural taboo which will involve a ritual process of accountability and reconciliation, the relationship between the father and son is not right. Even from the Christian perspective, Robert is not following the Christian values of "honor thy father and thy mother." There is also a need to explore the interpersonal relationships between Robert and the father.

Much work is needed to resolve issues of interpersonal relations between the Dzobo family and their extended families. The Dzobos seem to have intentionally severed these relationships, and only in hindsight have they come to realize the importance of these extended family ties. The fact that they are considered to have a "holier than thou" attitude toward others seems to get in the way of their family relationships. Their pastor is the person best equipped to help them realize how their attitude toward others has damaged their relationships.

The pastoral caregiver must encourage the Dzobos to explore issues of their conflicting interpersonal relations, and help them identify how evil and good operate in their lives. Questions such as the following must be raised: What is the meaning and quality of community for the Dzobos? What is their interpersonal relationship with God and what is their image of God? How is God's power perceived in their life story? Who or what is held responsible for their faulty communal interpersonal relations? What do they perceive as their part in the disruption of these faulty communal relations? With which Bible stories do they personally identify? How do the Dzobos use the Bible stories - negatively or positively - to justify their behaviors? In the final analysis, what issues of estrangement (from God and others), brokenness, forgiveness, accountability, justice, and restitution need to take place before the Dzobo family can feel whole again?

The pastoral caregiver can also help identify the Dzobos' experience of religious dissonance. However, a pastor working with the Dzobos, using the above questions, would allow and encourage the Dzobos to identify and name their experiences of the religious dissonance. The events taking place through Robert appear to be pointing to the *ngozi* spirit*'s* predictions. However, as Christians, the Dzobos are refusing to explore the possibility of facing this evil, as illustrated by the wife's statement that they are "covered by the blood of Christ." Exploring the possibility of this evil would mean the Dzobos would have to involve themselves in traditional

Shona rituals condemned by the church. In addition, it would mean the Dzobos would have to "swallow" their self-righteous pride and openly admit the possibility that their relationships with God and the Spirit World are not right either. The Dzobos need to be challenged in their belief that their family's "being covered by the power of the blood of Jesus" does not alter the fact that a possible evil committed by the deceased parents may need resolution.

The pastoral caregiver must explore with the Dzobos their understanding of the *ngozi* spirit. Is the *ngozi* spirit evil or good? Have they considered accepting as possible reality the idea of the presence of a *ngozi* spirit hounding their family? If it becomes a reality, what difference does it make, and what changes would they, as Christians, have to make in their lives? If the evil was committed, what would be right or wrong in engaging in a reconciliation process with the *ngozi* spirit and its family?

Suggested Pastoral Response. A pastoral caregiver with an integrative consciousness could employ different methods and approaches in helping this family. The pastoral caregiver could provide intensive individual caregiving with Robert, focusing on issues of identity confusion and his fear about parents dying, before they perform the ritual to resolve the *ngozi* problem. Robert also needs individual care in terms of drug abuse issues, as well as how that might be affecting his perceptions and his relationship with his family.

Another level involves the pastoral caregiver employing a communal approach in focusing on their communal interpersonal relations when exploring the issues affecting the entire family. With the pastoral caregiver's exploration of the socio-cultural influences, family members' anxiety and its source, and religious issues, it is the hope of this writer that the Dzobos will be willing to look from a different perspective at what is happening in their lives. The aforementioned process allows the Dzobo family to revisit their Christian beliefs and the Shona traditional values from which they have become estranged. The pastoral caregiver's comfortable willingness to explore issues such as these gives the Dzobos an invitation, as well as a "green light," to go ahead and be open to discussing issues they formerly had considered "untouchable." It encourages the Dzobos to revisit the Shona traditional rituals and reconsider how to resolve the issues. At the same time, what is important for the pastor is to understand the ritual to resolve the *ngozi* spirit problem, to be able to explain the process involved.

One of the main problems and core issues in the requirement for incorporating aspects of a traditional Shona ritual into the current Shona Christian rituals in place is the need to address the lack of relevancy and completeness in the latter. The Dzobo family needs to involve inclusion of aspects of traditional Shona ritual to resolve the *ngozi*. Why the suggestion of employing the ritual to resolve the *ngozi* in this case of the Dzobos? One of the main reasons to pursue the suggested ritual to resolve the *ngozi* situation is based on the traditional Shona religio-cultural beliefs in relationship to the occurrences in the Dzobo family. The *ngozi* spirit's announcement that Robert's grandparents would not live past the age of fifty (and they subsequently did die before fifty), and Robert's behaving as a *rombe*-someone who roams the streets exhibiting signs of mental illness, (which had also been announced by the *ngozi* spirit) are issues which defy an explanation of "coincidence" insofar as most Shonas with traditional Shona religio-cultural values (including the upper middle-class Shona Christians) are concerned.

The Western Christian ritual in use today (which recognizes the existence of a *ngozi* spirit as one which is evil) calls for an exorcism of the *ngozi* spirit, but does not incorporate the traditional methods used to address the avenging spirit via use of the Shona ritual components of accountability, restitution, and reconciliation. The Shona Christian church views the avenging spirit and its actions as evil because Western Christianity condemned it as evil and taught that humans (including spirits of dead persons) are not to avenge themselves; rather, the deceased human being or spirit is to leave the situation which it views as an injustice so that God can render justice. "Beloved, never avenge yourselves, but leave room for the wrath of God; for it is written, 'Vengeance is mine, I will repay, says the Lord.'" (Romans 12:19)[6] For the Shona Christian, however, the influences of the traditional world-view do not free him or her from the

6 Romans 12:19 *NRSV*.

psychological impact of relational theological understanding: that justice not only involves God's avenging on behalf of the victim, but involves reconciliation and justice-making rituals which involve the extended family, God, Spirit World (including the avenging spirit), and creation.

The pastoral caregiver in the role of the traditional medicine person has to ask the *ngozi* spirit to tell who s/he is and where her/his home is, relate the story about how s/he was killed and what happened after s/he was killed. The pastoral caregiver must ask the whereabouts of the bodily remains of the spirit, and whether they are buried. Included in this process are questions about the demands of the *ngozi* and how the *ngozi* feels accountability, restitution, and reconciliation can be justly meted. The pastor would also have to act as mediator between the families of the deceased and the murderer, throughout the entire process, which involves bringing the two families together, with the *ngozi* retelling its story and stating its demands. The family of the *ngozi* can add further demands, over and above those made by the *ngozi* spirit. Having done all that is required, the final phase involves forgiveness and reconciliation between the extended families. The closing ritual involves a meal shared by the families, as a sign of reconciliation. The payments of restitution are essential; otherwise the avenging spirit will not rest. At the closing of the reconciliation, the pastor must address the *ngozi* spirit, exorcize it, and ask it to leave the murderer's family in peace, since they professed accountability, paid restitution, and asked for forgiveness, and the families shared a reconciliation meal. If the deceased *ngozi* was not given proper burial, then both families will need to find the bodily remains and accord them a proper burial. The church did not want to have anything to do with this ritual and its use of a medicine person, in part because the process is too long and involving.

As mentioned before, I argue that an exorcism alone, which does not involve the full processes of justice-making observed from the traditional Shona religious understanding involving accountability, restitution and reconciliation, is a "solution" which victimizes the victim (the *ngozi* or avenging spirit). Simply employing the method of exorcism does not give any urban Shona Christian whose family is related to an offender (murderer) any psychological and spiritual comfort inasmuch as those related to the offender are aware that the *ngozi* spirit can attack their families through illness or other means, despite their Christian status, until the ritual is performed. The exorcism merely removes the *ngozi* spirit from one person to another within that extended family system, but does not stop the avenging spirit's justice-seeking activities by causing illness and sometimes even death to the family of the murderer. Hence, the way to stop the *ngozi* from avenging is to incorporate some of the traditional problem-resolving steps (as already mentioned) forbidden by Western Christianity in pastoral caregiving situations.

The church is also opposed to the involvement of the traditional medicine person in rituals such as that of an avenging spirit, since the church views the activities of the medicine person as influenced by the paganistic world-view. It is, however, not necessary to use a medicine person in this ritual; since the spirit is ostensibly already speaking through Robert, the pastoral caregiver can play the traditional role of the medicine person in the presence of the Dzobo family, with some of the church members as witnesses.

Desire for Another Child. *The case of Tsitsi, a married woman, who came to the pastor requesting prayer to help her conceive a child, is an example of a case in which the pastoral caregiver could blend Western individualistic approaches with some of the communal approaches to pastoral care. The couple involved already had a ten-year-old, and had been trying to have another child since the birth of the first. Tsitsi related to her pastor the story of her growing up with both a mother and grandmother who believed she was supposed to be a nun. Tsitsi was told by the mother never to get married (the mother said she had seen a vision of Tsitsi as a nun) but to dedicate her life to Christ, become a nun, and be used as God's instrument. When she was growing up, the mother used to examine Tsitsi to make sure she was still a virgin. Tsitsi's mother died of a heart attack at the age of 40. Tsitsi was 13 years old when she went to live with her grandmother in another village. The grandmother was more strict with Tsitsi as pertaining to religion compared to the deceased mother.*

The grandmother repeated the story of the vision told by the mother. In addition, she told Tsitsi since she was a chosen one to be a nun, if she ever had any sexual intercourse with a man she would never be able to stand the pain. Any intercourse would be as if a man was drilling with a hot iron through her vagina. Sex was dirty, and if Tsitsi was ever to have sex it would be painful as a punishment for disobeying. Tsitsi personally did not want to be a nun but developed a fear of having any relationships with boys. Tsitsi also had a dream in which she was a nun, and in the dream a voice told her she was a chosen one to serve Christ.

After the deaths of both the mother and the grandmother, Tsitsi moved to live with one of her aunts in the city. The aunt allowed Tsitsi to do all the things that the mother and grandmother had forbidden. Tsitsi's aunt allowed her to wear trousers and go to birthday parties and the boyfriend whom she was seriously dating when she was 19 years old was allowed to take Tsitsi to the movies as long as they got back home by 8:00 p.m. Tsitsi was surprised by all this freedom but always felt guilty whenever she went out with her boyfriend. She did not tell her aunt about the story the mother and grandmother had told her about becoming a nun.

When Tsitsi was 20 years old, the boyfriend asked that they take a drive to the mountains. Both Tsitsi and the aunt agreed that she could go. While out in the mountains, just before getting back home, the boyfriend insisted that they have sex. Tsitsi refused, saying she was not ready. The boyfriend being physically big, easily overpowered Tsitsi and raped her. Tsitsi said she cried and screamed, but since they were in the car and in the middle of nowhere, she knew there was no one who could hear her. She was bleeding and terrified. The boyfriend tried to comfort her after the act, but all she wanted was to go home. She reported, "It happened just the way grandmother and mother had told me." She felt as if someone was drilling a hot iron through her vagina. She said when the boyfriend was raping her, she could hear the voices of both the mother and the grandmother repeating how she had committed an unforgivable sin, that she was defiled, and that she would pay for it the rest of her life. When she arrived home, no one was there, and she went straight to her room and cried all night. When she tried to sleep, she would have a re-occurrence of her mother's and grandmother's voices. She could not bear the pain. She kept a cold towel on her vagina that night to numb the pain. Tsitsi said she prayed that night like she had never before, asking God's forgiveness. She finally fell asleep for two hours that night and when she awoke she was better, but was not herself most of that following day. The boyfriend came by to see her and she refused to see him.

After about a month Tsitsi found out she was pregnant. She told the boyfriend and the aunt, and she consented to get married. Within six months the two got married. Tsitsi said their wedding night was another "horror night." It was a replay of the day she was raped. The husband could not understand this, and Tsitsi could not gather enough courage to tell him her life story growing up with the mother and grandmother. She said every time for the past ten years, the only way the husband had sex with her was by forcing himself on her. Tsitsi said it is painful, but now she found out one way to deal with the pain was to leave her body and she could watch her husband having sex with her from above. She said she loves her husband, and wants another child, but just cannot bear the pain of having sex with her husband. Tsitsi said it is just like the grandmother said, "she would pay for the rest of her life," and she is paying. She says she is even ashamed to see her husband naked. They never take baths together and the husband always forces himself on her in the dark. After saying all this, Tsitsi looked tired but there was a lot of relief from her face.

Socio-cultural Issues. The importance of examining the socio-cultural issues in this case is to aid the pastoral caregiver with an approach which would be relevant in giving voice to Tsitsi and space to vent her pain. It helps the pastoral caregiver explore, at a cultural level, the degree to which Tsitsi might be comfortable exploring her issues as an individual without immediately involving the extended family system. The socio-cultural analysis also aids the pastoral caregiver in assessing how Tsitsi's cultural world-view affects her perspective on her interpersonal relations.

Tsitsi and her husband are an economically lower middle class family. The husband is familiar with both the African traditional religio-culture and Christianity. Tsitsi did not have as much exposure to African traditional religion and culture, but has some familiarity with it. The couple appears to be comfortable operating in both cultures. They visited a Western doctor who could not diagnose any medical reasons why Tsitsi failed to conceive a second time. On the other hand, since she had been brought up by a religiously strict Catholic mother and grandmother, Tsitsi mentioned she did not believe there were any related Shona traditional religio-cultural issues which were involved in her inability to have another child.

Tsitsi needs some work to resolve her relationship with her deceased mother and grandmother whom she feels she disobeyed. She has not disclosed to her husband the history of her upbringing, or the impact of the rape on their relationship.

Anxiety, its Sources, and Psychological Issues. One of the main tasks of the pastoral caregiver is to help Tsitsi become aware of the fact that much of her anxiety stems significantly from her sense of guilt about being married when she had been taught she was supposed to have been a nun. She believes that her experience of pain during sexual intercourse with her husband is a result of disobeying her mother, grandmother, and God's desire. Tsitsi feels anxiety for having disobeyed God, and believes that she will never be forgiven by God. She has prayed for all these years for another child, and she sees the fact that she has not been able to conceive as a sign from God that God hates her sin of disobedience. The experience of the initial rape itself put Tsitsi in a state of anxiety for all subsequent contact in which her husband initiates sexual intercourse with her. Tsitsi has to "make love" to someone who raped her and continues to do so.

In addition, the pastoral caregiver must work with Tsitsi on her feelings of anger toward God, the mother, the grandmother, and her husband. Tsitsi has anger against her husband mixed with her guilty feelings and is therefore unable to confront the husband about the rape. Questioning why she feels God is "punishing her" could reveal the source of her anger toward God. Tsitsi could be angry at her mother and grandmother for raising her the way they did, as well.

Psychologically, Tsitsi feels as though she is a misfit and rejected by God. She functions well in everyday life, but her marital relationship, and the guilt placed on her by her mother and grandmother, are emotionally and psychologically a constant burden. Tsitsi had lived, and continues to live, her mother and grandmother's prescription for her "contact." Due to the false teachings from the mother and grandmother, in addition to the rape incident, Tsitsi has developed a poor self-image.

The problem of vaginismus is a major one for her.[7] The explanation of vaginismus to Tsitsi, even though based on a Western perspective, will help relieve Tsitsi of some of her psychological burden and anxiety. Her understanding of vaginismus will help with the process of pursuing care and resolution. Tsitsi might gain additional insight from a female nurse who can explain vaginismus to Tsitsi and discuss how the rape impacted her physically, psychologically, and in her marital relationship.

Theological or Religious Issues. A pastoral caregiver with an integrative consciousness must be willing to explore with Tsitsi her religious world-view and work with her, starting from what she understands. Tsitsi expressed that she believes spirits can prevent conception (African traditional religious belief); however, she does not believe that there is any spirit preventing her from having another child. Tsitsi knows there is nothing which was ritually placed on her in childhood, to prevent her from conceiving. On the other hand, in the process of seeking reconciliation for Tsitsi with her deceased mother and grandmother, there is a need to explore whether Tsitsi might also think the spirits of her angry deceased mother and grandmother might be responsible for her inability to conceive. Every time she tried to sleep during the night of the initial rape, she reports having heard her mother and grandmother's voices telling her she had sinned. As much as one might try to reduce this phenomenon as a psychological trauma, it is also closely tied to the African traditional belief that the spirit of a dead person (living dead) can still influence or communicate with the living.

Tsitsi does not believe that God will forgive her, and believes that God is punishing her, a false idea she picked up from the misguided Christianity of her mother and grandmother. Tsitsi also quoted the Christian teaching

---

7 R. C. Carson, J. N. Butcher, and J. C. Coleman, eds., *Abnormal Psychology and the Modern Life* (Illinois: Scott, Foresman & Co., 1992). These authors say about vaginismus: ". . .women who suffer from vaginismus also have arousal insufficiency, possibly as a result of conditional fears associated with the traumatic rape experience . . ." (416).

of honoring one's parents, adding that she had failed to do so. There are questions of disobedience and punishment from the Christian point of view. Coming from a Catholic background, Tsitsi needs absolution from someone in authority who is in a priestly or pastoral office. Reassuring her that she did nothing wrong in not becoming a nun, that she is not living in sin with her husband, and that she is not under any punishment from God will give Tsitsi a sense of peace, a positive self-image, and a new sense of self-esteem.

Suggested Pastoral Response. This is a case in which a pastor with an integrative consciousness can employ or utilize the Western approach to pastoral care while paying particular attention to the African traditional religious themes that may arise. There are many psychological issues that need to be addressed. Here the Western approach of first engaging individual pastoral care will be more plausible than the Shona traditional group or community oriented approach.

Tsitsi's individual experiences have shaped her life and can be approached from her unique and specific point of view. The issues with which she is dealing require addressing Tsitsi as an individual before involving others with her in pastoral care. Before Tsitsi can expose her experiences to others, she must confront them and deal with them in the presence of someone she trusts. She has never opened her life story to anyone other than the pastor. In short, I am arguing that Tsitsi needs to do the bulk of the work with the pastor before other people are introduced to the pastoral care process. However, before the process of care is completed with the pastor, her husband and possibly the aunt will need to be involved. The husband has to hear Tsitsi's story, and there is a need for reconciliation between the two of them in terms of the issues of date rape.

The pastoral caregiver might also want to encourage Tsitsi to relate her life story to her aunt, so she can have another female hear her pain and receive reassurance of the fact that her pain is not imagined. As mentioned above, a female nurse can also help explain the vaginismus to her, and continue to work with Tsitsi on how to desensitize her body to that pain. She is dissociating while having sexual intercourse with her husband, and must be taught that this phenomenon is one way her mind is dealing with the pain emotionally, psychologically, and physically.

The pastoral caregiver must work diligently to persuade Tsitsi that she did not sin against God by not becoming a nun. In addition, she needs to understand the source of the pain (vaginismus) which she experiences while having intercourse with her husband. In the final analysis, the question of prioritizing the issues of interpersonal relationships or estrangement (from God and others), brokenness, forgiveness, accountability, justice, and restitution need to be resolved before Tsitsi can feel whole again.

Generational, Cultural and Religious Conflict. *Nhamo and Netsai are a young couple in their thirties. They live in one of the suburbs of Harare. Nhamo is a very independent man who has assimilated many Western cultural and economic values and who owns a very successful business. The couple decided to consult their pastor after continual illness of their son, difficulties in their marriage, and the husband's depression.*

Their problems started when Nhamo went to introduce Netsai to his parents. Nhamo's father openly rejected Nhamo's intentions to marry Netsai. Nhamo's father said he had heard that Netsai's family was accused of being witches and that the family was being hounded by a ngozi spirit. Nhamo asked his father to reconsider.

At the family meeting, Nhamo's father restated his reasons for refusing to approve of Nhamo's proposed marriage. Nhamo became angry and started to speak in English. The uncles and grandfather registered their complaint that they felt disrespected by Nhamo, and could not help him since he was speaking in English. He told them they (including his father) were not Christian and were not educated enough. The father told Nhamo he had a grudge against him and that he was disowning Nhamo. Nhamo proceeded to marry Netsai. When the couple moved into their suburban home they found a horn filled with blood, hanging in a tree next to their bedroom window. They invited some church members to help them burn the horn. The horn, however, did not burn.

The couple's first pregnancy ended in a miscarriage, despite Netsai's having received prenatal care. Zvitendo (now three years old) was born from the second pregnancy but is a sickly child. At one point, when Zvitendo was seriously ill, the couple went to several European doctors, and were told by one of the English medical doctors that the root cause of the illness of their son was traditional, "zvechivanhu." What the doctor meant was that the solution could be found in the Shona traditional religious culture. He advised them to look for a traditional medicine person. Nhamo responded that they would not seek the help of a medicine person since they were Christians and that Christ would see them through all their problems. However, after the visit, the wife secretly took the son to a traditional medicine person. The medicine person in his "kushopera," the traditional casting of the divining bones-told the wife that he saw that there was a "wandering spirit" and that something was wrong within the family relations of both of the couple's families of origin. He said he could only give details of the problems if Netsai's husband was present. The medicine person prescribed "muti," medicinal roots for Netsai to give to the child. The child appeared to respond positively after two days of being on the prescribed medicine from the medicine person. Prior to the medicine he used to sleep only three to four hours and would then wake up the rest of the night due to the nightmares. Unlike in the past, he slept throughout the night after Netsai gave him the "muti."

A week after Netsai's visit to the medicine person, Nhamo found the "muti" (medicinal roots) prescribed for the son and he threw them away. That same day Zvitendo could not sleep. Nhamo told his wife that he did not want his wife going to visit with her family anymore because he was convinced that they were the ones who had influenced her to see the medicine person. In addition, he also accused Netsai's family of not being Christian, of being poor and lazy, and of milking him of his wealth. Netsai's relatives needed to realize Nhamo had big medical bills to pay to get his son well. He was tired of taking care of "a whole village," he said. Netsai shared this with her aunt who, in turn, shared the story with Netsai's family of origin. Netsai's family responded, "Achazviona, anodada netuhupfumi twake itwotwo. Ukama hunopfuura hupfumi. Akaona tichitsika kumba kwake atibvunze." This translates to mean, "He will have to face it, he is proud of his small riches. Relationships are more important than wealth. Let him ask us if he will ever find anyone of us paying him a visit again."

Nhamo also told his wife that her act of visiting the medicine person could be grounds for divorce and that she was a backsliding Christian. Netsai told Nhamo what the medicine person had said and that the medicine person wanted to meet with Nhamo as well. Nhamo responded by saying, "Not even over my dead body would I consult a medicine person."

During this time, word also reached them that Nhamo's father was seriously ill. Nhamo started having re-occurring dreams and nightmares of his father dying without having set things right with him. The couple noticed that the days when Nhamo's depression was better the son was ill the most and vice versa. Zvitendo started having terrible nightmares. The son talked about seeing a horn, a frightening ugly human-like figure and hearing a voice during the nightmares. The voice said that Zvitendo would suffer the rest of his life to pay for his father's deeds. This caused Nhamo to be even more depressed, and he also continued to have re-occurring dreams of the father dying without reconciliation. In the dream Nhamo's father's spoke the words "ndikafa zwinhu zwakadai uchazviona," which translates as "if I die with things the way they are (conflicted relationship) Nhamo would have to face the consequences."

Nhamo became depressed and would not go to work or to church. At this point they decided to call the pastor, who was a young man, serving his second year in the ministry as a lay pastor. The young pastor was someone who had been born and raised in the city, and who had not received any pastoral training. He did not believe in the Shona traditional world-view. The first time the pastor heard about the couple's situation through "the grapevine," he used the couple's situation as an illustration during a worship service saying he had heard that there were some members of the church who had visited a medicine person. In his preaching he condemned "those members" in front of the congregation as being weak in faith and headed for hell and condemnation.

Socio-cultural Issues. The socio-cultural analysis of Nhamo and Netsai helps the pastoral caregiver in assessing the main cultural influences affecting both of them, and determining how these influences have affected their interpersonal relationships. Nhamo is someone who has assimilated Western cultural values, is a successful business person, and focuses on economic success rather than on his communal interpersonal relationships. Nhamo grew up in the mission schools where he was prevented from assimilating the Shona traditional religio-culture. He acts more Western than Shona. Nhamo functions at the level of naive consciousness. He has assimilated Western values to the extent that he does not analyze when to apply those Western values. He speaks to his grandfather and uncles in English, despite the fact that they have told him they do not understand the English language.

Due to the crisis in his family, Nhamo now realizes that the Western socio-culture of economic success cannot provide him with the support he now needs. He has money, but the money is not providing him with the sustenance of an extended family support system. Nhamo is also now experiencing cultural dissonance.

The couple loves their son, but have no other relationships other than their nuclear family. Nhamo has spent a lot of money on the treatment of his son. The son's illness is a factor in the severance of relationships with the extended family and in Nhamo's subsequent focus on the nuclear family. In addition, the couple has been condemned by the church as people of weak faith. This has also left them with a poor support system in terms of their church family.

Anxiety, its Sources, and Psychological Issues. The pastoral caregiver can explore at least three different sources of Nhamo's and Netsai's anxiety. First, Zvitendo's illness appears to be one of the main sources of anxiety for the couple. The nightmares Zvitendo is experiencing appear to be pointing to something Nhamo did which involves the African traditional religio-culture, which Nhamo vehemently despises as pagan and heathen. The wife went to a *nganga* (medicine person) with their son, Zvitendo. The medicine she was given for Zvitendo appeared to work, and the wife was told to bring her husband to the *nganga* for further information. Consulting a medicine person is one of the things Nhamo is opposed to, but now he appears to be in a dilemma, after hearing what the son is telling them about the nightmares. During the nightmares, the spirit asks why Nhamo burned his "stuff." The solution points to Nhamo having to shift his beliefs and accommodate some of the African traditional beliefs and solutions. The church already condemned them as a lukewarm Christian family. As much as Nhamo condemns African traditional beliefs, he does not know what to do with the situation surrounding his son's, and his own, illness. The doctors have not been able to diagnose the cause of Zvitendo's illness. The illness has shaken the grounds of Nhamo's Christian faith, and the church has not provided him with the type of support system he expected during this time of need. The doctors and his Christian faith have not been able to provide him with solutions to the problems, and Nhamo is anxious about the idea of having to look for resolution in that which he condemns as pagan and heathen. In short, Nhamo is experiencing religious dissonance.

Second, the pastoral caregiver must explore with Nhamo the issue of his father's illness, and how their faulty dysfunctional relationship is affecting Nhamo. Nhamo has constant dreams of his father dying without having reached reconciliation with him, which is another source of great anxiety. Nhamo realizes there will be added consequences if his father dies without reconciliation being achieved. He does not know how to go back and address the situation of his broken relationship with his father.

The third source of Nhamo's anxiety which the pastoral caregiver can help address is his broken interpersonal relationships with the extended family. The extended family members from Netsai's family side have vowed never to step in Nhamo's home again. They have told Nhamo that his foolishness lies in failing to realize that relationships are more important than riches. It is Nhamo's behavior and words which severed his relationship with his own family of origin, including his extended family members. He condemned their Christian beliefs as "lukewarm," and said he did not need anyone except Christ.

Netsai's anxiety is based on lack of control. She has been condemned by her husband and the church for going to the medicine person. In addition, she is not allowed to have any relationships with her extended family. She has not been able to free herself from oppression in this marriage. Netsai's beliefs (consulting the medicine person) have been condemned by both the church and her husband, even though she is convinced that the medicine prescribed by the medicine person for their son was working. I agree with ma Mpolo that the caregiver must explore the problem from the careseeker's point of view. He notes:

> As a starting point, the therapist should accept as valid the experience of the patient. This therapeutic encounter lowers the distance separating the patient and the therapist. By accepting the diagnosis of the patient, his/her world view is at the disposal of the therapist who, with analytical mind, can explore it in depth.[8]

Netsai has never been given an opportunity to tell her story and what she believes about Zvitendo's illness. Netsai needs to be allowed to present her point of view. The pastoral caregiver must be attuned to psychological issues with which this couple are struggling and examine how they pertain to the issues of bi-culturalism and bi-religiousness. Netsai does not appear to have any problems mixing the two religions, Shona traditional religion and Christianity. Nhamo, on the other hand, is totally opposed to Shona traditional religion. That to which Nhamo is opposed appears to be what works, insofar as was proven by the useful medicine Netsai got from the medicine person for Zvitendo.

Nhamo and Netsai seem to be caught between issues of success within their relationships. This has caused them much misery inasmuch as they have become an "island unto themselves." They cannot seem to fit well with the Western nor the Shona traditional culture. As stated earlier, this has created anxiety in terms of a lack of an available support system. Psychologically, they are struggling with a lack of both cultural and spiritual grounding. They have no "home" psychologically or culturally. The two now feel isolated. The Christian foundation they have always depended upon appears to have been shaken. In addition, Nhamo is depressed and confused, and appears to be questioning his religious beliefs.

Religious or Theological Issues. The pastoral caregiver utilizing an integrative consciousness must be attuned to the different diagnoses being given by Nhamo and Netsai. One of the main religious issues with which this family is faced relates to the cause of Zvitendo's illness, which the doctors have been unable to diagnose. Coupled with the physical illness

---

8 ma Mpolo and Kalu, eds., *The Risk of Growth*, 5.

and Zvitendo's nightmares (which in the Shona religious understanding are an indication of an unsettled spirit of a dead person who needs recognition or reconciliation), Nhamo's problem is that he does not entertain or allow any Shona traditional religio-cultural values to be mingled with his Christian beliefs. Nhamo appears to be in a significant struggle insofar as acknowledging the power of the spirit, since he considers such a belief an influence of the pagan world. The pastoral caregiver must explore whether Nhamo might feel that a diagnosis of Zvitendo's illness, as related to an influence of a spirit hounding him, would be condemned as an indication of shallowness in Nhamo's own Christian faith. He also may fear being viewed as a weak or unfaithful Christian, due to the perception that his family is being attacked by the pagan powers.

Nhamo's nuclear family's relationship with the spirit is an issue which needs to be addressed, since it appears to be directly related to Zvitendo's illness. It is easy to conclude from the Shona traditional world-view that Nhamo cut down a tree which might have ritually been given as a home to a spirit. Nhamo burning the "stuff"-the container with a horn filled with blood, was a mistake. There is a high possibility that the "stuff" belonged to the previous owners of the house, and Nhamo could have consulted with them and let them take their "stuff," if it belonged to them. If the previous owners of the house were not associated with the container, Nhamo could have asked the help of other Christians to ritually remove the "stuff" and request that the spirit move elsewhere, since they did not know the spirit or have any relationship with it. They did not need to burn the container. By attempting to burn the container, Nhamo committed a violation against the spirit. Some form of acknowledgment or reconciliation needs to happen between Nhamo's nuclear family and the spirit.

Nhamo needs to be questioned about what be believes about the "spirits." The best place to start may be to refer him to the Biblical stories referring to when Christ was casting out evil spirits from people. It is not unchristian to believe that evil spirits exist. The questions about Nhamo's biblical images or stories with which his family identifies need to be explored. How are these biblical stories being used or misused in Nhamo's and his family's experience?

There are also issues of communal interpersonal relationships between Nhamo's family, the church, and God. In addition, Nhamo must address issues of his interpersonal relationships with his wife, father, and the general extended family on both sides. Both are seeking healthy interpersonal relationships.

At this moment of crisis, Nhamo and Netsai need to explore their interpersonal relationship with God. Where do they see God at work or not at work in their lives? What needs to change pertaining to how they perceive God? Is God wrathful and unforgiving? Is God punishing them by making Zvitendo sick? Does Nhamo perceive belief in the power of an evil spirit as something God will judge him for as an unforgivable sin? Could God use the Shona traditional methods (not contrary to Christianity) to help heal Zvitendo? Nhamo and Netsai need to re-examine the ways in which they relate to God, and explore ways God could bring healing to their family.

Netsai's and Nhamo's marital relationship needs attention. Netsai needs the freedom to tell her story and articulate her religious beliefs. How does it feel for her to be married to Nhamo? How does it feel for her to have been condemned by both the church and her husband? How is she handling the fact that she is not allowed to have any contact with her extended family? What does she wish could change? Netsai is to be given the freedom to narrate how she feels about Zvitendo's illness, and to express her opinions regarding viable solutions to the illness.

The issue of the relationship with the church or congregation is one which is hard to address. If a pastor with an integrative consciousness is involved in such a case, the person to work with first would ideally be the local pastor of Nhamo's church. The local pastor must fully understand that his condemnation of his parishioners in a sermon, without having provided pastoral care to them, was a poor approach. The first thing the local pastor was supposed to do was to meet with the couple and hear their story. The pastor with an integrative consciousness can work on theological, religious, and pastoral care issues with the local pastor. This provides the local pastor an opportunity to realize his mistakes and work with the couple differently. If the local pastor takes the lead in providing Nhamo's family with a sense of welcome and tolerance, the congregation may be encouraged to follow and grow in their own understanding and beliefs.

The pastoral caregiver's next task for Nhamo and Netsai involves working on their relationship with the extended families. The starting point lies with Nhamo's father, since he is in very poor health. Nhamo must swallow his pride and ask for forgiveness for the things Nhamo said to his father. Nhamo has to realize that his father's belief in some things from the traditional religion does not mean he is "not Christian enough." Nhamo used his own Christian ways as the yardstick with which to judge his parents. In addition, there was no reason for Nhamo to disrespect his father by telling him he was an uneducated man. The source of Nhamo's dreams could well be a manifestation of his guilty conscience about his relationship with his father.

Nhamo needs to realize that his assimilation of Western values and Christianity appears to have gravely interfered with his relationship with his father and his extended family. As someone who is educated, Nhamo appears to exhibit a naive consciousness in that he does not analyze the situation and context and subsequently apply the best approach. The same inadequate naive approach was applied by Nhamo in the way in which he responded to his uncles and grandfather, telling them they were "lukewarm Christians." Christianity does not promote passing judgments on other people's Christian beliefs and values.

Nhamo needs to comprehend that his "holier than thou" attitude toward extended family members is the main problem impeding the progress and success of his communal interpersonal relationships. It is Nhamo who needs to take the first step of asking for forgiveness. He needs to learn what Christianity says about forgiveness and relationships with both Christians and non-christians. If Nhamo's relationship with his family and other Christians is not right, can it be right with God? From the Christian understanding, Nhamo can be encouraged to engage in a process of rebuilding his relationship with his extended family. Jesus set a process of forgiveness in which one goes to the person who has committed sin, before offering a gift at the altar if he/she remembers the fault; then, to leave the gift at the altar, go and resolve the issue and so forth (Matthew 5:21-25).[9]

Nhamo and Netsai need help to explore issues around Zvitendo's illness, their communal interpersonal relationships with God, the spirit world, extended family relations, and with their church family. The process will also help Nhamo and Netsai re-evaluate their Christian values, as well as their marriage relationship. In the final analysis, the question of interpersonal relationships or estrangement from God, spirit world and others, brokenness, forgiveness, accountability, justice, and restitution need to be resolved before Nhamo's and Netsai's family can feel whole again. What van Beek, a pastoral counselor and theologian, concludes about the clash of worldviews in one of his case analyses holds true to Nhamo's and Netsai's situation. He says:

> The clash of meaning providing processes has reached a crisis point. They are riddled with guilt, plagued by fear, and jolted by anger. . . Worldviews rub against each other like crusts of land riding on restless continental plates. Everything is affected, the way they see the other, themselves, the people who raised them, the God they believe brought them together so irresistibly.[10]

Suggested Pastoral Response. In this case, one of the main tasks of the pastoral caregiver is to help Nhamo and Netsai realize the need for reconciliation between them and the spirit which is appearing to Zvitendo in the form of a nightmare. The action Nhamo and his friends from church performed in attempting to burn the container is the rightful ritual acknowledged by the Shona Christian church today. Since this action brought not peace, but rather more psychological and spiritual chaos to Nhamo's family, I am proposing an alternate solution which incorporates aspects from the traditional Shona world-view. The basis or criterion of the alternative solution is based on Shona traditional relational theology, which recognizes that, by burning the container, a violation was done to the spirit by Nhamo and his church friends. The spirit's home (the tree) was cut without announcement. Since the spirit is talking through Zvitendo's

---

9 Matthew 5:21-25 *NRSV*.

10 Aart M. van Beek, *Cross-Cultural Counseling* (Minneapolis: Fortress Press, 1996), 45.

nightmares, the spirit can be asked what it wants, who ritually placed it in the tree, and what is needed for reconciliation to be reached. After such a ritual, the spirit can then be exorcized and sent forth to its rightful relatives.

The pastoral caregiver must also take the lead in helping Nhamo and Netsai address their interpersonal relationships with their extended families. The family gathering(s) will allow opportunities for those with grievances against Nhamo to air them. Since there were no previous strong relationships between the two families, this might also provide an opportunity for the families to begin a better relationship. To a certain extent, Nhamo will be used as a scapegoat in the process; however, this will also bring to the fore unresolved issues which the families can identify and pursue in the hope of eventual reconciliation.

A Case of Polygamy. *Mr. and Mrs Moyo are in their old age. Mrs. Moyo is in poor health; she is asthmatic and has heart problems. Mrs. Moyo was the first one to suggest that her husband get another wife: her niece, Rudo. After menopause, due to a cultural belief she holds, Mrs. Moyo stopped engaging in sexual intercourse with Mr. Moyo. She argued that Rudo would be of good help to them, and Mr. Moyo would also have a stable wife. Mrs. Moyo is afraid that her husband could be tempted by an indecent woman and could perhaps contract AIDS or other sexually transmitted diseases. Rudo is a forty-year-old teacher.*

Mr. Moyo tried to convince his wife that her beliefs involving sex after menopause were cultural and had no scientific basis. He took her to a white male young medical doctor to discuss the disease. This made Mrs Moyo more adamant, saying the doctor was young, she (Mrs. Moyo) was not White, and that White doctors did not understand or know about some of the African diseases. Mrs. Moyo did not waver from her beliefs.

Two months after the visit to the doctor, Mrs. Moyo's niece, Rudo moved in with them. Mrs. Moyo talked to Mr. Moyo and to Rudo separately, wondering whether the two would be interested in each other. Rudo has always had a "crush" on Mr. Moyo, and has indicated she would be interested in the marriage, if she had her aunt's blessing. Initially, Mr. Moyo was opposed to the idea, since this is contrary to Christian standards. There is no sexual relationship between Mr. Moyo and Rudo, but the issue of marriage has been raised. The extended family members approve; however, the Moyos' church does not allow polygamy, and they are perceived by the church members as role models. They sought help from their pastor.

Socio-cultural Issues. The Moyos are an affluent couple who live in a suburban home. Mrs. Moyo converted to Christianity in her thirties, after having been raised by parents who were African traditionalists. While Mrs. Moyo is a very strong Christian, she also has high respect for Shona traditional values, as evidenced by her beliefs about sexual intercourse past menopause. In addition, she does not seem to have any objections to her husband marrying another wife, which she knows is contrary to Christian teachings, yet is also culturally acceptable.

The Moyos honor their extended family ties. Before going to consult with the pastor, they consulted with both sides of their respective extended families, to seek their blessings. Neither family had any problems accepting a second marriage, and left the final decision to be made by Mr. and Mrs. Moyo. In addition, the couple also consulted with their children, who voiced support for a second marriage, but realizing their parents' Christian values, asked Mr. and Mrs. Moyo to make the final decision themselves. The Moyos' communal interpersonal relationships appear to be healthy.

Regarding the issue of polygamy, the main issues raised today by most African women theologians and other writers primarily involve men's desire for power, control, and oppression of women. The Moyos' case does not clearly bring those particular issues to the surface. Mrs. Moyo initiated the idea of Mr. Moyo marrying a second wife; Mr. Moyo himself initially opposed the marriage.

Because of her health problems, Mrs. Moyo realizes she needs Rudo's help, as well as procuring someone who can fulfill her husband's sexual needs which Mrs. Moyo feels she can no longer meet. Rudo is a forty-year-old educated woman and a self-supporting primary school teacher. She is not being forced into the marriage, but rather sees it as an opportunity to help her aunt, and at the same time become married to someone she loves. In short, the general issue of man's need of power and control, common in most polygamous marriages, is not apparent in this case. It appears the idea of a second marriage was reached with the full and voluntary involvement of the three people who would be the major figures in the marriage. In this case, Mrs. Moyo took the leading role, choosing to initiate the second marriage.

Anxiety, its Sources, and Psychological Issues. The main source of anxiety for the Moyos is the prospect of participating in a polygamous marriage, a lifestyle contrary to Western Christian teachings. The Moyos are considered role models in the church they helped start, and becoming polygamous would have a detrimental effect on the life of the church. This would mean Mr. Moyo would have to relinquish his leadership position in the church and forfeit the right to bring forth for baptism any children born to his second, polygamous marriage. Even though it is culturally acceptable, religiously and theologically this is something perceived as contrary to the Christian teachings of the Moyos' church, hence, the anxiety.

Mrs. Moyo appears to be psychologically accepting of the entire situation. Some of her feelings may be based on her level of comfort with issues involving the Shona traditional culture. When she converted, she did not try to do away with most of the Shona traditional cultural beliefs. On the other hand, Mr. Moyo is caught between Shona religio-cultural beliefs and the Western Christian beliefs. His Western Christian beliefs have posed a psychological conflict for him. He has been a role model for the church, and engaging in polygamy sets a bad example. How is he going to fit into the congregation with two wives? Will it mean changing churches? And what would the act of changing churches say about his Christianity? The fact that Mr. Moyo has agreed to take the step to consult the pastor about this issue appears to indicate that he is beginning to question the religious beliefs involving polygamy and is anxious about engaging in it without the pastor's counsel or blessing.

Rudo does not appear to have any problems with the prospective marriage. One could also argue that the fact that she already had a "crush" on Mr. Moyo has clouded her critical judgment about marrying Mr. Moyo. She does not appear to be caught in the psychological dilemma of whether this is Christian or unchristian. She appears to have a clear conscience about her decision, and awaits her aunt's blessing.

Religious or Theological Issues. I recognize that I am not the first one to attempt to address the general issue of polygamy in Africa. With this awareness, I will utilize other people's views in the analysis of this case. There are several aspects of polygamy this author may not pursue in greater detail, such as the analysis of polygamy as a system oppressive to women, and the socio-economic basis of polygamy in the Shona traditional society.[11] These are all important issues which need to be addressed when discussing polygamy. However, as stated earlier, in the Moyos' case the focus of this analysis does not appear to bring these issues to the surface.

At another level, I argue that some polygamous marriages are better than monogamous ones. There are some Shona Christians who are involved in monogamous marriages in which the husbands are oppressive and behave in ways as unchristian-like as can be imagined. If the church's stance contends that polygamous marriages are oppressive, why does the church fail to discipline such oppressive monogamous men in the same manner as the polygamous men?

One could also argue that the appearance of apparent peace in these polygamous marriages is due to the submissive nature of the women involved; in short, they are not truly happy. Still, this author is convinced that there are some Shona polygamous marriages which would meet all the Christian standards of being a Christian family. Those involved in the polygamous marriages cannot be considered fully Christian simply because of the type marriage in which they live. The argument for or against polygamy in the Shona Christian church can go either way. I however, also argue that justice and issues of equality in a marriage are not automatic simply because the marriage is monogamous.

I find myself in a dilemma; having observed some of the injustices and oppression within some polygamous marriages, I also struggle with advocating for polygamy in the Shona context. However, cases such as that

---

11 Adrian Hastings, *Christian Marriage in Africa*, (London: SPCK, 1974), see also Hatendi, "Shona Marriage and the Christian Church,"135-149.

of the Moyos or cases in which a polygamous man converts to Christianity and is forced to divorce all but one wife, and cases involving peaceful responsible polygamous men who participate in the life of the church but who are not given all the rights and privileges awarded other church members, force this writer to challenge the church to re-visit this issue.

In addition, in the West, as much as polygamy is legally prohibited, it is common knowledge that it still exists in states such as Utah. The other irony in the West is that polygamy is prohibited but, what has been commonly termed *serial polygamy* is flourishing. Serial polygamy is where a man marries and divorces as many times as they want. The question of who is more Christian a *serial polygamist* who marries and divorces more than five wives or a responsible polygamist who is committed and happily married to his two wives. From my opinion, serial polygamy encourages lack of commitment in marriages. Many will go into the marriages with the mind set that if the marriage does not work they will divorce and marry someone else. I am neither advocating for women nor men staying in abusive hellish marriages. Wonder why the divorce rate in the USA has always been higher than most countries? I believe this is one of the reasons in my opinion. Examples of Christian prohibitions involving polygamous men include: denial of full membership in the church, no freedom to hold a church office (all polygamous United Methodist men have probationary membership in the church), forbidding polygamists to bring their children forth for baptism, and denying them the right to be accorded a full Christian burial ritual.

The theological and religious issues this author would focus on in the analysis of this case are related to the question of whether polygamy is wrong for all Christians. Are polygamous people less Christian and less valuable in the eyes of God? Why can polygamous people not be accorded the full membership rights of other Christians? The focus will be primarily on the theological and religious issues precipitated by polygamous marriages in the African context, and more specifically in the Shona context.

Most polygamous Christian converts were ordered to divorce all their second and subsequent wives, and to remain only with the first wife in order to participate fully in the life of the church. The coming of

Christianity, in that respect, created many broken homes, with newly divorced and disenfranchised women and their children forming many new single parent homes. One could ask, what is more sinful, breaking up a home or letting someone remain polygamous, take care of his family, and raise all his children together with all his wives, living within the dictates of Christian morals?

Muzorewa, a Shona theologian, sees the change taking place in matters of polygamy as more economically based, and of course, due to Christian influence on the Africans. He notes:

> Over a few decades, the African breadwinner began to feel that a large family was not an asset but a financial burden in a cash economy. This new attitude was a clear departure from the traditional view that cherished a large family. Thus, the institution of the family was immediately affected by the presence of Christianity as it was presented in Western garb. Polygamy was despised by the missionaries so much that African converts began to condemn it too. In fact, present-day missionaries like Aylward Shorter still insist that monogamy, and not polygamy, is the Christian ideal. . .But such a claim is classified as backward; worse still, it is labeled unchristian.[12]

The opposition to polygamy by missionaries was contrary to what Africans found in the Bible. When they read about the God-fearing men and famous leaders such as David, Solomon, and many others, it led to the breaking away and founding of so-called "Independent" or "Indigenous" churches in many countries on the continent. Why did the missionaries label polygamy a sin or wrong when great and faithful men such as David were not condemned for it? Even our forefather Abraham had two wives. The Old Testament is very close to the culture and religious beliefs of the African people; it therefore would support the African understanding of polygamy. The Western interpretation of Jesus' teaching about marriage is understood differently by many Africans.

There are many arguments posed regarding what Jesus meant in the gospels about marriage, especially Mark 10:6.[13] First, after Jesus quoted Genesis, he did not conclude by saying "therefore polygamy is a sin."

---

12 Muzorewa, *The Origins and Developments of African Theology*, 31-32.

13 Mark 10:6 *NRSV*.

Second, "the two shall become one flesh" is a phrase used even by Paul in reference to being united in sexual intimacy. Paul uses the same verse to warn man against prostitution. He says, "Do you not know that he who joins himself to a prostitute becomes one body with her? For it is written, 'The two shall become one flesh.'" (1 Corinthians 6:16-17).[14] The phrase "the two shall become one flesh" has been used to justify monogamy. However, based on this biblical language, it does not translate to a simple mathematical problem (such as 1x1=1), as most Westerners interpret this verse. The "one flesh" is understood by most Africans (especially those who advocate polygamy) to mean the unity that takes place between a man and a woman in the intimate and sexual relationship.

A third argument which could be posed is that the verse Jesus quotes is out of the book of Genesis, at the beginning of creation. Interestingly, after God said, "A man leaves his father and his mother and cleaves to his wife, and they become one flesh" (Genesis 2:24), many men, including Abraham, went ahead and married more than one wife, and were not rebuked, condemned, nor punished for it.[15] No prophet in the Bible preaches against polygamy as a sin. Why has it become a sin today for one to be polygamous? Is this not something adapted by the Western community to fit their cultural and social beliefs, and then baptized into Christianity? One could also say there were definitely polygamous people during Christ's time; instead, Jesus did not address the issue of polygamy but of marriage, as aforementioned.

Augsburger, a Western pastoral theologian, makes a good point when he notes:

> Since marriage and family are such varied human structures, any theology of marriage and the family must address a world of institutions. . .Polygamous societies in Africa and polyandrous societies in the Himalayas have their own ethics; extended families in the East have their own traditions and values. . . Such marriages are not loose multiple associations but stable parallel unions contracted

---

14 1Cor 6:16-17 *NRSV.*

15 Genesis 2:24 *NRSV.*

> under communal law, recognized as marriage by the society, entered with lifelong intentions, and providing a permanent context for offspring.[16]

This aforementioned point by Augsburger makes a good theological argument for any type of a marriage contract, as long as it is sanctioned, approved, and blessed by the society. Many times there is a tendency for people to judge others' behaviors and culture as out of norm, based on their own.

Polygamy has been said by many Christian churches, including the Shona United Methodist church, to be a sinful and inferior type of marriage. This is not biblically based, yet is the Western norm Christians are expected to follow. Augsburger again notes the following about what he thinks most Christians around the world have been lead to believe about polygamy:

> 1. Polygamy is unacceptable. It is simply a sin comparable to adultery.
> 2. Polygamy is an inferior form of marriage, not sinful where it is the custom but always unacceptable for Christians.
> 3. Polygamy is a form of marriage less satisfactory than monogamy and one that cannot do justice to the full spirit of Christian marriage but one can still put up with it, as they put up with slavery, dictatorial government, and much else. Existing multiple marriages can be accepted while monogamous change is invited.[17]

What the missionaries thought, and what the present Shona Christian church still thinks is best for the Shona Christian people, involves doing away with polygamy, breaking families, and causing significant psychological burdens to those Christians who found (or find themselves today) in such relationships.

To turn back to the Moyos' case, there is no biblical basis for arguing theologically against Mr. Moyo marrying a second wife. If Mr. Moyo was to pose this question, the answer for Mr. Moyo would be to respond that monogamy is a religious belief which has been followed by the Christian

---

16 D. W. Augsburger, *Pastoral Counseling Cross Cultures* (Philadelphia: Westminster Press, 1986), 206-207.

17 Ibid., 209.

church and which has been standardized into a Christian tradition. Within the Shona context, where Independent churches welcome polygamy, Mr. Moyo could also ask the question of whether those Independent Christian church members are less Christian for marrying more than one wife. Mr. Moyo could ask whether polygamy would make him less Christian, and if he remained strong in his Christian beliefs and practices, would God not accept him as God's child? Mr. Moyo needs to be openly told that Independent Christian church members are not less Christian, and that Mr. Moyo would not become less Christian, nor would God reject him for marrying a second wife.

Again, monogamy is a Christian practice established by the church for the purposes of order and conduct of its members, but polygamy is not biblically condemned as a sin. Augsburger argues that there is no clear biblical basis upon which to condemn polygamy. Bearing this point in mind, he raises the question: "Does the pastoral counselor facilitate persons acting in a more loving way within the accepted structures of the particular society? Or does effective pastoral care require a critique or rejection of some structure and the innovation of others?"[18] The answer to the questions raised by Augsburger about the work of the pastoral counselor (in this case, the pastoral caregiver) is to facilitate relationships within acceptable structures of the Shona society. In places where the structures are oppressive and unjust, it is the work of the pastoral caregiver to critique or reject such oppressive structures. Augsburger goes further, making a strong point against undoing some family structures using a single theological and biblical model:

> Biblical and theological studies that seek to offer a single model for families violate the rich diversity present in two thousand years of biblical history. A theology of the family that seeks to deal inclusively with the biblical diversity is best expressed in paradoxical truth rather than in propositional truth.[19]

---

18 Ibid.

19 Ibid., 210-211.

The Shona pastoral caregiver must struggle with theological justification versus the problems inherent in condemning polygamy theologically, even as the church adamantly promotes monogamy. Mr. Moyo must be informed of the consequences, and be made aware that his subsequent loss of the right to participate in Christian church sacraments is not based on the scriptures but rather is based on precepts designed to bolster and confirm the order of the church.

Dickson, an African theologian from Ghana, cites the case of a similar situation in Ghana, stating how polygamous man are not accorded full burial rights and their bodies are not allowed to enter the sanctuary. However, the ritual read at the graveside recognizes the deceased polygamous man as one who "had faithfully lived, and faithfully died."[20]

A similar circumstance would happen to Mr. Moyo if he chose to marry a second wife. Would Mr. Moyo's polygamy make him less Christian, and therefore warrant that his body, upon death, be denied interment from the church he helped create? The irony of the situation is that, before death, such people are allowed to enter the sanctuary, but as soon as they are dead their (dead) bodies cannot enter that same sanctuary.

Suggested Pastoral Response. I can see at least two prospective ways in which to approach this case. First the pastoral caregiver could provide intensive pastoral care, focused on the Moyos' maintaining their present marriage. This would mean working with Mrs. Moyo to change her cultural beliefs about sexual intercourse after menopause. One prospect would involve bringing in a married Shona female nurse or perhaps a woman pastor, of the same age as Mrs. Moyo, who is still engaging in sexual intercourse with her husband, to counsel Mrs. Moyo. The reason Mrs. Moyo may have ignored the white male doctor's advice to continue sexual intimacy could be her suspicion that he was not well invested in women's issues, let alone Shona cultural matters. However, if Mrs. Moyo is firmly entrenched in this cultural belief, change to this belief system might not be an option. One has to observe great caution in trying to change cultural

20 K. A. Dickson, *Theology in Africa* (London: Doarton, Longman and Todd, 1984), 105.

beliefs since this has significant and far reaching psychological effects if the beliefs are changed without a solid base upon which to fall back.

The suggested inclusion of a nurse is based on the nurse's knowledge of feminine physical, emotional, and medical issues. Impact would be maximized if the nurse was someone Mrs. Moyo knew, and was also a member of her own church. It could be someone Mrs. Moyo already trusted, who could talk to with her openly about her fears, and would at least facilitate valid and beneficial communication.

Mr. and Mrs. Moyo have been able to live for the past ten years without having sexual intercourse with each other. How have they been handling the situation of sexual abstinence? Are there other preferred alternatives which might be satisfying for Mr. and Mrs. Moyo, in the absence of traditional sexual intercourse? It is also necessary to explore whether cultural beliefs are the sole reason for the cessation of sexual intercourse between the Mr. and Mrs. Moyo. How has the issue of Mrs. Moyo's health played a role in the relationship? The Moyos are an affluent family and can afford to hire help to do the housework and so forth, if her health is the key issue.

Another alternative (not available in the Shona urban church) is to honor the views of the Moyos. If polygamy becomes their primary alternative, then there are several areas to be addressed. As much as both Mr. and Mrs. Moyo appear to be leaning toward the second marriage, the pastoral caregiver has to explore the following with the Moyos: What is the main reason which brought them to the pastor for care? Is it Mrs. Moyo's failing health, or the impaired sexual relationship, or perhaps another reason - alone or in combination with the other possibilities? Have their current beliefs about polygamy changed compared to the past? If so, how and why? In addition, how is the idea of a second marriage affecting their present marriage relationship? How do the Moyos foresee their relationship with other church members? Might other church members begin to treat Mr. Moyo as a weak Christian? Even though he is endeavoring to be open about his feelings, the reaction from most of the congregation could be to point fingers of blame rather than extend help and understanding to him.

In addition, how do the Moyos see their relationship with God, and with their extended family, in the event of a second marriage? What are some of the biblical stories with which they identify? How are these biblical stories construed or perhaps misused by the Moyos? Are there issues of guilt as to how they perceive God's love, following the second marriage?

Issues surrounding the impact of the second marriage on the Moyos' primary relationship need to be considered. What is the role of a second wife? What about issues of jealousy? In the Shona culture, the first wife is treated as the "host" wife, which literally means she has more power than the second wife. The issue of power and control between the two women needs special attention. In short, what are the pros and cons of having a second wife in the marriage? A positive factor that is to the advantage of the Moyos in this situation is the fact that both know Rudo well and seem to respect and accept her.

In addition to the relationship between the two women, Mr. Moyo's relationship with both women must be explored. How is Mr. Moyo going to treat the two wives equally? If Rudo is going to provide that which Mrs. Moyo is currently unable to provide (sexual intercourse), what does that mean for Mrs. Moyo senior? Is Rudo's job mainly to provide sexual intimacy or does Mr. Moyo truly love her? These questions would help the Moyos explore ideas and feelings about their future relationship.

This aforementioned alternative is one which helps those exploring the possibilities of a polygamous marriage to reach their decision, informed of the pros and cons. This option is not available in the contemporary urban Shona Christian context. The church's stance is: no polygamy, period. I am proposing that, with cases such as this one involving the Moyos, the Shona church could provide such an option.

The pastoral caregiver is according respect to cultural beliefs, and working from the careseeker's context, to include whatever new information may become available to the careseeker. Western knowledge (new information) is useful, but must not be forced on the careseeker, since this may counter the progress in pastoral care. All the cases point to the need for considering communal interpersonal relations in the contemporary urban Shona context. The urban Shona Christians need a new pastoral care approach in helping parishioners resolve their crisis experiences.

CHAPTER SIX

An Integrative Pastoral Theology of Care: Implications for Theory and Practice

This concluding chapter has two subsections focusing on the theory and practice of pastoral care in the urban Shona context. The first part addresses the implications for education and training of pastoral caregivers serving in the urban Shona context. The second section focuses on the implications for practice of care in this context.

This book has argued that for a pastoral theology of care to be relevant in the contemporary urban Shona Christian context, pastors or pastoral caregivers serving in this context must be equipped with a pastoral theological and psychodynamic understanding of integrative consciousness. Integrative consciousness means that a pastor must possess knowledge of, or easily comprehend, both Shona and Western world-views, as well as the blending and integration of aspects of Shona and Western world-views in personal or religious identity formation and/or in providing care.

Implications for Education and Training of Pastoral Caregivers

What are the implications for education and training in pastoral methodological approach to pastoral care in the urban Shona context? I suggest the following five implications for the Shona context in pastoral methodological approach.

1) First and foremost, the church needs to create rituals pastors can be trained to use in serving in the contemporary urban Shona context. These

are rituals which integrate both traditional Shona religious rituals and Western Christian rituals and are intended to replace those currently in use. The integrative rituals then can be sanctioned by the church for use in the training of and utilization by the urban Shona pastoral caregivers.

What this implies for pastoral care methods in the urban Shona context is similar to the proposal by Patton in pastoral theological method in pastoral care. He notes:

> The second-order language of theology is distinguished by critique and comparison. It examines the essential religious meanings growing out of the first-order language and experience (. . .in story, hymn, or ritual express the way an individual or community affirms its relationship with God) and compares them with the beliefs of particular community of faith. In that process, theology further explicates and reinterprets the doctrines of the community in relation to ongoing religious experience of the first order.[1]

The urban Shona context needs Patton's type of approach. The currently used rituals and theology, operative in the urban Shona context, are first-order and need to be reinterpreted in order for them to be relevant. Most of the rituals and doctrines in place do not always address the issues of the urban Shona bi-religious experiences, so there is a need for critique and reinterpretation of these rituals.

In addition, curriculum for training pastoral caregivers needs to incorporate the use of the proposed new rituals. Raising the issues regarding the need for integration of rituals in the urban Shona context, and analyzing the old rituals, helps raise trainees' consciousness to the ways rituals are inadequate and sometimes non-liberating. As Patton says: "Awareness of the tension between oppression and liberation in the institutions and ideologies of the communities that shape human lives and of which one is a part. . ." is one of the goals of pastoral theology and care.[2]

2) The training and education of pastoral caregivers serving in the urban Shona context calls for caregivers to be conscientious about the need

---

1 John Patton, *Pastoral Care in Context: An Introduction to Pastoral Care* (Kentucky: Westminster/John Knox Press, 1993), 237-238.

2 Ibid., 241.

for methodological flexibility in those providing care. Sole use of Western methods in approaching care issues is inadequate since most Western theories of pastoral care are individualistic in approach and are sometimes contrary to the urban Shona context in which many people are still in flux within their individual or communal orientation. At the same time, employing traditional Shona approaches to pastoral care alone does not suffice, due to the influence of Western Christianity and Westernization. Hence, the need exists for a pastoral approach which is flexible and takes into account the aspects which influence the pastoral careseeker's world-view and values.

van Beek, a Western pastoral counselor and theologian, notes the following about the importance of world-view:

> Worldview entails the way people judge the world around them, including what is beautiful or despicable, what is moral and wrong, what is wise and foolish, what our rights, as well as our responsibilities, are. The list goes on. But worldview also determines how people view themselves and the community of which they are a part. Conversely the family community, and society in which we belong to a large extent determine our worldview.[3]

Starting with what is known by the careseeker (in terms of world-view and religious and cultural values) helps in terms of establishing rapport, and creates common ground upon which the pastoral caregiver and careseeker can connect.

All the case studies presented indicated the need for flexibility in the method of the caregivers' approaches. Only Tsitsi's case could utilize much of the Western individual approach in pastoral care, yet it still requires minimal integration from the traditional methods. The other three cases require an integration of methods, especially in the rituals.

The lack of communal interpersonal relationships for the upper middle class urban Shona calls for training of pastoral caregivers which can tap into the traditional approach in care (group or communal oriented care). This requires pastors to be trained and to acquire some expertise in reorganizing their congregations into support groups for those experiencing

3 van Beek, *Cross-cultural Counseling*, 43-44.

similar problems in personal or religious identity confusion. This way the parishioners can share their stories and realize that they are not alone in their struggles. At another level, the pastoral caregivers must be trained to teach their congregations to provide support and a sense of a community of embeddedness for their parishioners.

3) The pastoral caregiver in the urban Shona context needs to be trained and educated in a method of analysis which utilizes a critical consciousness. This reflects an ability to analyze situations beyond the presenting problem. It requires hermeneutical skills with which to analyze situations that are influenced by two cultures and two religious world-views, and to avoid naive value judgments which can impede providing adequate care.

Since the urban Shona experiences conflict in religion and culture, it is also necessary that the pastoral caregiver be able to identify the particular sources of anxiety inasmuch as there might be more than one source of anxiety resulting from the tension within and between the cultures and religions. Identifying the sources of anxiety will in turn help identify the anxiety itself. The ability to detect the careseekers' experiences with cultural and religious dissonance aids in assessing the anxiety and its sources. The goal is to help the careseekers learn to identify multiple world-views and manage their anxiety so it does not stifle their self understanding.

4) The urban Shona pastoral caregivers need education and training which make them aware of the experiences of identity confusion within the urban upper middle class, resulting from colonization and the persistent influence of Western culture versus the influence of the traditional Shona cultures. The pastoral caregiver needs education and training that will help him/her point out factors (such as lack of communal support and economic pressures) which contribute toward personal identity confusion in the urban Shona society.

Cultural and religious dissonance creates identity confusion. The work of the pastoral caregiver is not to re-create a "traditional Shona identity" in careseekers, but is rather to help minimize the level of anxiety resulting from the identity confusion. The pastoral caregiver may recommend the need for the careseeker to explore communal interpersonal relations as a way to correct his or her (careseeker's) identity confusion. van Beek also notes about individual identity:

> Knowing that identity does not develop on its own, we could say that identity is a plant that can flourish only in the soil of belonging. The idea of being able to "find oneself" by separating from the belonging group may be popular in contemporary North American society, but it may be largely a fallacy. How can we know who we are if we do not belong anywhere? [4]

This calls for the pastoral caregivers to be equipped through appropriate training in conscientizing (without being judgmental) or socializing those struggling with issues of personal identity who come seeking care . Furniss calls this task of pastoral care, "adult socialization":

> Pastoral care, understood sociologically, is a type of adult socialization. We often think of socialization only as the process by which children are changed from human animals to social beings. Yet learning and developing new skills are life long processes. Socialization is any structured social relationship for purposes of enhancing learning, coping, and developing new attitudes and perspectives. . . When pastoral care does a good job of helping careseekers understand their choices, it facilitates people's learning in a striking way.[5]

In this case, those struggling with issues of personal and religious identity can be socialized by helping them understand their choices in terms of issues of personal and religious identity confusion.

5) The urban Shona context requires that the pastors be trained or equipped with the ability to utilize relational pastoral theological methods of care. As discussed in Chapter Four, a relational pastoral theology is one which pays attention to individuals' narratives in connection to their communal interpersonal relationships with other individuals, God and creation. In the traditional Shona context, broken relationships cause much anxiety. The traditional world-view, condemned as heathen by the church, still influences the urban Shona people. Dismissing the Shona traditional

---

4 Ibid., 57.

5 George M. Furniss, *The Social Context of Pastoral Care: Defining the Life Situation* (Kentucky: Westminster John Knox Press, 1994), 56.

religious world-view, or simply labeling traditional rituals as heathen or pagan practices, may overlook some of the issues of communal interpersonal relations which might be a cause of breakdown in relations.

Implications for the Practice of Pastoral Care

The practice of pastoral care in the urban Shona context, as already alluded to in the above section on training, requires that pastoral caregivers utilize a diversity of methods. This, therefore, requires flexibility in the modalities of providing care. In providing care in the urban Shona context the pastoral caregiver must be attuned to the following five issues in order for care to be effective.

1) Narratives (stories) come naturally to most Africans. Even many of the upper middle class urban Shonas still use narratives to relate their problems to the caregiver. In some cases, the narratives may be presented in the form of a traditional fairytale, story, or sometimes using Shona proverbs or sayings. A pastoral caregiver has to probe to get beyond the surface meaning of these stories, or needs to be able to analyze the story, so as to understand what the careseeker derives from the story or proverb.

Directly connected to the narratives are Biblical stories with which the careseekers identify. It is the work of the caregiver to explore how these stories are being used by the careseeker. Are the biblical stories being used for ill or for good? Are there ways in which to give positive meaning to the stories if they are being applied negatively in the careseeker's life?

2) The pastoral caregiver must be attuned to issues of communal interpersonal relations, or the lack of them, in the narratives. How are the careseeker's interpersonal relationships? Are the interpersonal relations, or lack of same, the source and cause of the anxiety he/she might be experiencing? The analysis of the interpersonal relations involves the family, church, the community at large, God, and creation.

3) The pastoral caregivers must be attuned to both the cultural and the religious world-views of the careseeker. Has the careseeker assimilated many of the Western cultural values at the expense of the traditional Shona values? Does the careseeker feel culturally connected or lost? Is the careseeker feeling a sense of cultural dissonance or confusion? How is the

culture, with which he or she does or does not identify, related to his/her identity confusion? Does the careseeker move between world-views (Western and traditional Shona), or feel caught between cultural world-views? Or is he or she grounded in one but borrows from the other?

The same analysis applied to the cultural world-view is important in addressing the religious world-view of the careseeker. Some careseekers move back and forth between the practices of Western Christianity and traditional Shona religion. Are the religious world-views and values mainly influenced by Western Christianity, the traditional Shona religion, or by both? The pastoral caregiver must be attuned to issues of bi-culturalism, bi-religiousness, or religious and cultural dissonance.

4) The pastoral caregiver must be attuned to the type of diagnosis given by the careseekers in any situation, especially where illness, death, or spirits are involved. Even after being given a Western diagnosis as to the cause of an illness, some upper middle class Shona Christians, as in the traditional Shona context, will still seek answers which involve traditional explanations for an illness. ma Mpolo notes:

> Etiology and diagnosis in the context of traditional African thought poses the following basic questions: "Who is the cause of my illness?" In this context, organically manifested symptoms are always the result of some external aggression. What is essentially sought in every illness, either somatic or emotional, is significant of such disease.
>
> Therefore, diagnosis was always synthetic in that it searched for, and announced, the cause of illness by providing its socio-psychological and spiritual significance. The consequences of such illness for the individual and the community were also indicated. [6]

The pastoral caregiver must be attuned to the world-view held by a careseeker and not too readily dismiss it as heathen. In other words, the caregiver must start from the careseeker's point of view and explore with him/her the meaning of the diagnosis and other alternative explanations.

5) The pastoral caregivers must be attuned to the careseeker's sense of community of embeddedness or lack thereof. Is the careseeker's community of embeddedness based out of the church community, in a

---

6 ma Mpolo & Kalu, eds., *The Risk of Growth*, 9-10.

community geared toward economic success, or within their extended family or their nuclear family? It is important to understand the careseeker's community of embeddedness because that community provides him/her with values, culture, and a sense of personal and religious identity. Furniss notes, regarding the value and function of one's reference group, which is similar to the community of embeddedness:

> The group whose definition of the situation constitutes a plausibility structure for the person's worldview is called her or his *reference group*. There are many possible reference groups available in the pluralistic society, and the one we choose as ours has major implications for our self identity.
>
> Pastoral care, as the exploration with careseekers of the possibility and implications of religious definitions of their situation, is crucially involved with the dynamics of reference group behavior and resulting social identity.[7]

Similar to what Furniss describes above about a reference group, the community of embeddedness provides the basis and values for one's religious and cultural context during times of crisis.

Conclusion. In conclusion, this book has argued that colonization, Western Christianity, and the continual influence of urbanization and Westernization have created a context of personal and religious identity confusion in the urban Shona context. As a result of this bi-culturalism and bi-religiousness, a different type of pastoral caregiver is needed to relevantly serve the needs of the urban Shona population which is caught in the experience of religious and cultural dissonance. The lack of communal interpersonal relations creates identity confusion and anxiety for most Christians who live in the urban Shona context. As demonstrated in the analyses of these cases, it is this writer's argument and conclusion that those pastoral caregivers serving the contemporary urban Shona context need to possess an integrative consciousness, which includes an awareness of both the Shona and Western world-views and which integrates both.

I agree with Sullivan's theory which postulates that what brings wholeness to one's personal identity is right interpersonal relations. In the Shona context, right relationships involve right communal interpersonal

---

7 Furniss, *The Social Context of Pastoral Care*, 37.

relationships with others, including the Spirit World. Within the Shona context, acts such as murder bring disharmony to the whole community. In such circumstances, rituals and ceremonies play a central role in bringing about healing to the entire community.

Alienation and estrangement, whether in relationships or with regard to one's culture of embeddedness, create anxiety and the need for pastoral care for those living in this urban Shona context. When individuals' interpersonal relationships feel disjointed, and they develop a sense of alienation and estrangement from the community, from God, and from others, rituals are needed to recapture the necessary sense of wholeness, as demonstrated in the case studies.

Pastoral care processes in the Shona Christian churches need to integrate some of the Shona traditional religious methods or rituals in order to be appropriate. The church has failed to initiate good credible progressive work in integrating some of the Shona traditional rituals which would minimize the anxiety arising from the bi-religiousness in which the urban Shona Christians find themselves. Finally, the pastoral caregiver in the urban Shona urban context must possess an integrative consciousness, a consciousness able to comprehend both the Western and the traditional Shona religion and culture and the integration thereof to br effective and relevant to the context.

BIBLIOGRAPHY

Acton, R. "A Colonial Childhood: Coming of Age in Rhodesia." *The North American Review* 272 (June 1990): 9-14.

Ajani-ya-Azibo, D."Towards a Metatheory of the African Personality: Incorporating an African World View into Psychology." (Special Issue) *Journal of Black Psychology* 17 (Spr. 1991):37-45.

Akbar, Na'im. *Chains and Images of Psychological Slavery*. New Jersey: New Mind Productions, 1984.

Akin-Ogundeji, O. "Some Thoughts on the Relevance of Applied Psychology in Africa." *International Journal of Psychology*. 22 (1987): 483-491.

Allport, Gordon. *Personality: A Psychological Interpretation*. New York: Henry Holt, 1937.

Anchin, J. C. & Kiesler, D. J. Eds. *Handbook of Interpersonal Psychotherapy*. New York, NY: Pergamon Press, 1982.

Appiah, Anthony. *In My Father's House*. New York: Oxford Press, 1992.

Appiah-Kubi, K. "Religion and Healing in an African Community: the Akan of Ghana." in L. Sullivan ed. *Healing and Restoring*. (1989):203 -224.

Appiah-Kubi, K., and S. Torres, (Eds.) *African Theology En Route.* N.Y.: Mayknoll Orbis Books, 1977.

Aschwanden, H. *Karanga Mythology: An Analysis of the Consciousness of the Karanga in Zimbabwe*. Gweru: Mambo Press, 1989.

Augsburger, D. W. *Pastoral Counseling Across Cultures*. Philadelphia: Westminster Press, 1986.

Banana, C. S. *Come and Share:An Introduction to Christian Theology.* Gweru, Zimbabwe: Mambo Press, 1991.

Baumeister, R. F., *Identity: Cultural Change and the Struggle for Self.* New York: Oxford University Press, 1986.

Beach, D. N. "The Initial Impact of Christianity on the Shona: the Protestants and the Southern Shona." In Dachs, A., (Ed.), *Christianity south of the Zambezi*. Gweru: Mambo Press, 1973.

Bediako, K. "The Roots of African Theology." *International Bulletin of Missionary Research* 13 (Apr. 1989):58-62.

Bell, C. *Ritual Theory and Ritual Practice.* New York: Oxford University Press, 1992.

Berends, W. "African Traditional Healing Practices and the Christian Community." *Missiology* 21 (Jul. 1993): 275-288.

Berinyuu, A. A. *Towards Theory and Practice of Pastoral Counseling in Africa.* N.Y.: Peter Lang, 1989.

______. "Change, Ritual and Grief: Continuity and Discontinuity of Pastoral Theology in Ghana." *Journal of Pastoral Care* 46 (Sum 1992): 141-152.

Bodian, Stephan. "Is Psychotherapy a Waste of Time." in *The Yoga Journal*. (May/June, 1992): 50.

Boulaga, E. *Christianity Without Fetish*. N.Y.: Maryknoll, Orbis Books, 1984.

Bourdillon, M. F. C. *The Shona Peoples: An Ethnography of the Contemporary Shona With Special Reference to Their Religion*. Gweru: Mambo Press, 1991.

______. *Where are the Ancestors: Changing Culture in Zimbabwe*. Harare: University of Zimbabwe Publication, 1993.

Boyd-Franklin, N., *Black Families in Therapy: A Multisystems Approach*. New York: The Guilford Press, 1989.

Buecher, H. *Spirits and Power: An Analysis of Shona Cosmology*. Cape Town, South Africa. Oxford University Press, 1980.

Capps, D. *Pastoral Care: A Thematic Approach*. Philadelphia: The Westminister Press, 1979.

Carson, R., and J. N. Butcher, Coleman, J. (Eds.) *Abnormal Psychology*. Illinois: Scott Foresman and Co., 1988.

Carter, J. D. & Narramore, B. *The Intergration of Psychology and Theology: An Introduction*. Grand Rapids, MI: Academie Books, 1979

Cesaire, Aime. *Discourse on Colonialism*. (English edition) New York and London: Monthly Review Press, 1972.

Chidyausiku, P. *Broken Roots: A Biographical Narrative on the Culture of the Shona People in Zimbabwe*. Gweru: Mambo Press, 1984.

Chikara, F., and M. R. Manley. "Psychiatry in Zimbabwe." *Hospital and Community Psychiatry* 42 (Sept, 1991): 943-947

Clinebell, H. *Basic Types of Pastoral Care and Counseling.* Nashville: Abingdon, 1984.

Couture, Pamela D. & Hunter, Rodney. eds *Pastoral Care and the Social Conflict*. Nashville: Abingdon, 1995.

Csordaa, T. J. "Healthy and the Holy in African, and Afro-American Spirit Possession." *Social Science and Medicine* 24 (1987):1-11.

Dachs, A. ed. "Traditional Religion in Shona Society." In *Christianity South of the Zambezi*, 11-24. Gweru: Mambo Press, 1973.

Dale, J. R., and D. I. Ben-Tovim. "Modern or Traditional? A study of Treatment Preference for Neuropsychiatric Disorders in Botswana." *British Journal of Psychiatry* 145 (1984):187-192.

Daneel, M. L. "The Encounter Between Christianity and Traditional African Culture: Accommodation or Transformation?" *Theological Evangelica* 12.3 (Sept. 1989): 36-51.

______.*Old and New in Southern Shona Independent Churches Vol.1.* The Hague: Mouton, 1971.

Deng, F. M. "Identity in Africa's Internal Conflicts." *American Behavioral Scientists*: 40 (Sept/Oct.1996): 46-66.

Dershimer, R. A. *Counseling the Bereaved.* New York, NY: Pergamon Press, 1990.

Dickson, K. A. *Theology in Africa*. London: Doarton, Longman and Todd, 1984.

______. "African Theology: Origin, Methodology and Content." *Journal of Religious Thought* 32 (Fall/Win. 1975): 34-45.

Dillard, J. *Multi-Cultural Counseling.* Chicago: Nelson Hall, 1983.

Dooyeweerd, Herman., *A New Critique of Theoretical Thought. Vol. IV.* Philadelphia: U.S.A. The Presbyterian and Reformed Publishing Co., 1969, 164.

Dubois, W. E. B. *The Souls of Black Folk*. New York: New American Library, 1969.

Dueck, A. "American Psychology in Cross-Cultural Context." *Journal of Psychology and Theology* 11 (1983):172-180.

Edards, S. D. et. al., "Traditional Zulu Theories of Illness in Psychiatric Patients." *Journal of Social Psychology*: (121) 1983:213-221.

Ela, J. *African Cry*. Maryknoll, N.Y.: Orbis Books, 1986.

Erikson, E. H. *Identity and the Life Cycle*. New York: International University Press, 1959.

______. *Childhood and Society*. 2nd ed., New York: W. W. Norton and Company, 1963.

Eugene, U. "Notes on Methodology for an African Theology." *AFER* 19 (Je. 1977):155-164.

Fanon, F. *The Wretched of the Earth*. New York: Grove Press, 1963.

______. *Black Skin White Masks*. New York: Grove Press, 1967.

Forde, D. (Ed.) *African Worlds: Studies in the Cosmological Ideas and Social Values of African People*. Great Britain: Oxford University Press, 1991.

Fortes, M. and G. Dieterlen. *African Systems of Thought*. London: Oxford University Press, 1960.

Freire, P. *The Pedagogy of the Oppressed.* Translated by Myra Bergman Ramos, New York: Continuum, 1983.

Freud, S. *The Problem of Anxiety.* Translated from the German by H. A. Bunker. Albany, NY: The Psychoanalytic Quarterly Press, 1936.

______. *New Introduction Lectures on Psychoanalysis.* Translated by J. H. Sprott. New York: W. W. Norton & Company, Inc., 1933.

______. *The Standard Edition of the Complete Psychological Works of Sigmund Freud.* (Pre-Psycho-Analytic Publications and Unpublished Drafts) Volume I (1886-1899). General Editorship of J. Strachey, Anna Freud. London: The Hogarth Press, 1966.

______. *A General Introduction to Psychoanalysis.* Authorized English Translation of the Revised Edition by J. Riviere and E. Jones. Garden City, NY: Garden City Publishing Co. Inc., 1935.

______. *An Outline of Psychoanalysis.* Authorized translation by James Strachey. New York: W. W. Norton & Company Inc., 1949.

Fry, P. *Spirits of Protest: Spirit-mediums and the Articulation of Consensus Among the Zezuru of Southern Rhodesia (Zimbabwe).* London, England: Cambridge University Press., 1976.

Furniss, G. M. *The Social Context of Pastoral Care: Defining the Life Situation.* Louisville, KY: Westminister John Knox Press., 1994.

Gelfand, M. *The Spiritual Beliefs of the Shona.* Gweru: Mambo Press, 1977.

______. *African Background: the Traditional Culture of the Shona Speaking People.* Cape Town: Juta & Company Limited, 1965.

______. "Psychiatric Disorders as Recognized by the Shona." In *Magic, Faith and Healing: Studies in Primitive Psychiatry Today*, ed. A. Kiev New York: Free Press, 1974: 60-74.

______. "African Perspective on Pastoral Theology: A Contribution to the Quest for more Encompassing Models of Pastoral Care."*The Interdisciplinary Journal of Pastoral Studies* 112 (1993): 3-12.

______. *The Witchdoctor: Traditional Medicine Man of Rhodesia (Zimbabwe)*. London: Harvill Press, 1964.

______. *Growing up in Shona Society: From Birth to Marriage*. Gweru, Zimbabwe: Mambo Press, 1971.

______. *The Genuine Shona: Survival Values of an African Culture*. Gweru: Mambo Press, 1973.

______. *The Shona Religion*. Gweru: Mambo Press, 1962.

Gilkes, C. T. "Colonialism and the Biblical Revolution in Africa." *Journal of Religious Thought* 41 (Fall/Win. 1985): 59-75.

Goba, B. "Toward a Quest for Christian Identity: a Third World Perspective." *Journal of Black Theology in South Africa* 2 (1988): 31-36.

Gombe, J. M., *Tsika dzaVaShona*. Harare, Zimbabwe: The College Press (Pvt) Ltd., 1986.

Graham, L. K. "From Psyche to System." *Theology Today.* 49 (Oct 1992): 320-333.

______. *Care of Persons, Care of Worlds: A Psychosystems Approach to Pastoral Care and Counseling*. Nashville: Abingdon, 1992.

Hall, C. S. & Lindzey, G. *Theories of Personality*. New York, NY: John Wiley & Sons, Inc. 1957.

Hamutyinei, M A. *Tsumo Namadimikira.* Gweru: Mambo Press, 1984.

Hannan, S J. *Standard Shona Dictionary.* (Rev. ed.) Gweru: Mambo Press, 1994.

Haviland, W A. *Cultural Anthropology*. (7th Ed.) Fort Worth, TX: Harcourt Brace College Publishers, 1993.

Heider, F. *The Psychology of Interpersonal Relations*. New York, NY: John Wiley & Sons, Inc., 1958.

Helgesson, A. *Church, State and People in Mozambique*. Uppsala: International Tryck AB., 1994.

Hernstein J. R., & Murray, C. *The Bell Curve: Intelligence and Class Structure in American life*. New York: Free Press, 1994.

Hesselgrave, D. *Counseling Cross Culturally*. Grand Rapids: Baker House, 1984.

Hiltner, S. *Preface to Pastoral Theology: The Ministry and Theory of Shepherding*. Nashville: Abingdon Press, 1978.

Hunter, R., ed. *Dictionary of Pastoral Care and Counseling.* Nashville: Abingdon, 1990.

Idowu, B. J. *African Traditional Religion*. Maryknoll, N.Y.: Orbis Books, 1975.

Ikenga-Metuh, E. "Towards an African Theology of Man." *Africa Theological Journal* 11 (1982): 143-150.

Imasogie, Osadolor. *Guidelines for Christian Theology in Africa.* Achimota, Ghana: African Christian Press, 1983.

Jahn, J. *Muntu: An Outline of the New African Culture*. New York: Grove Press Inc, 1961.

Jones, A. "Psychological Functioning in Black Americans: A Conceptual Guide for Use in Psychotherapy." *Psychotherapy* 22 (1985): 363-369.

Jongh van Arkel, J. T. de. "Teaching Pastoral Care and Counseling in an African Context: A Problem of Contextual Relevancy." *Journal of Pastoral Care* 49 (Sum. 1995): 189-199.

Kabore, G. The Importance of Self-Image. *UNESCO Sources* 79 (May 1996): 14.

Kabweza, M. "Teaching Religion to the Shona." *AFER*: 23 (June,1981): 138-141.

Kahari, G. P. "Missionary Influences in Shona Literature." In *Christianity South of the Zambezi*. ed. M. Bourdillon. 2 (1977): 87-102.

______. *The Search for Zimbabwean Identity*. Gweru: Mambo Press, 1980.

Kalilombe, P. "The Salvific Value of African Religions." *AFER* 21.3 (June 1979): 143-155.

Kapenzi, G. Z. *The Clash of Cultures: Christian Missionaries and the Shona of Rhodesia.* Washington, D.C.: University Press of America, Inc. 1979.

Kegan, Robert. *The Evolving Self: Problem and Process in Human Development*. Cambridge: MA, Harvard University Press, 1982.

Khoapa, B. A. *The African Personality*. Tokyo Japan: The United Nations University, 1980.

Kiev, A. *Magic, Faith, and Healing: Studies in Primitive Psychiatry*. New York: Free Press, 1966.

Kileff, Peggy and Clive. eds., *Shona Customs: Essays by African Writers.* Gweru: Mambo Press, 1992.

Lagerwerf, L. *Witchcraft, Sorcery, and Spirit Possession: Pastoral Responses in Africa.* Gweru: Mambo Press, 1992.

Lambo, T. Adeoye. "Mental Health of Man in Africa." *African Affairs* vol 80, (319), April, 1981, 278.

Lartey, E. Y. *Pastoral Counseling in Intercultural Perspective*. New York: Peter Lang, 1987.

LeVine, R. A. "Patterns of Personality in Africa." *Ethos* 1 (1973):123-152.

Lloyd, P. C. *Africa in Social Change: Changing Traditional Societies in the Modern World.* Baltimore: Penguin Books Inc., 1967.

ma Mpolo, M. & Kalu, W. *The Risk of Growth: Counseling and Pastoral Theology in the African Context*. Nigeria: Daystar Press, 1985.

ma Mpolo, M. and D. Nwachuku. *Pastoral Care and Counseling in Africa Today*. New York: Peter Lang, 1991.

Mafuba, Chemist. "Children Risk Losing Mother Tongue, Culture." *The Herald,* Monday June 17, 1996: 22.

Magesa, L. *African Religion: The Moral Traditions of Abundant Life.* NY: Maryknoll, Orbis Books, 1997.

Maimela, S. S. "Salvation in African Traditional Religions." *Missionalia.* Vol 13, No. 2, (Aug, 1985): 67.

Makura, T. *Vatete Vachabvepi*. Gweru, Zimbabwe: Mambo Press, 1976.

Manyambiri, F. *Akafa Apenyu*. Gweru: Mambo Press, 1990.

Marsella, A. J., and B.P. Pedersen, eds. *Cross Cultural Counseling and Psychotherapy*. New York: Pergamon Press, 1981.

Martey, E. *African Theology: Inculturation and Liberation*. N.Y.: Maryknoll, Orbis Books, 1993.

Martin, Denis-Constant. "Out of Africa! Should we be Done with Africanism." In *The Surreptitious Speech Presence Africaine and the Politics of Otherness 1947-1987*, ed. V.Y. Mudimbe. Chicago and London: University of Chicago Press, 1992.

Mbiti John S. *African Religions & Philosophy*. 2nd Ed. Portsmouth, NH: Heinemann Publishing. 1997.

______.*Concepts of God in Africa*. New York, NY: Praeger Publishers, 1970.

______. *Introduction to African Religion*. 2nd Ed. England: Heinemann International Literature and Textbooks, 1991.

______. *Bible and Theology in African Christianity*. New York, NY: Oxford Press, 1986.

Mbuy, T. H. "The Need for Pastoral Care of Youth in Africa." *AFER* 38 (1996): 2-10.

McFadyen, A. I. *The Call to Personhood: A Christian Theory of the Individual in Social Relationships*. Cambridge, England: Cambridge University Press, 1990.

McIntosh, I. F. *Pastoral Care and Pastoral Theology*. Philadelphia, PA: The Westminister Press, 1972.

Mead, M. *Growing up in New Guinea.* New York, NY. William Morrow & Co., 1953.

Mead, G. H. *Mind, Self and Society*. Chicago: University of Chicago Press, 1934.

______. *The Individual and the Social Self.* Edited with an Introduction by D. L. Miller. Chicago, IL: The University of Chicago Press, 1982.

Memmi, Albert. *The Colonizer and the Colonized.* Boston: Beacon Press, 1991.

Merwe van der, W. J. *The Shona Idea of God.* Fort Victoria (now, Masvingo): Morganister Mission Press, 1957.

Metuh, D. E. I. *God and Man in African Religion: A Case Study of the Igbo of Nigeria*. London, England: Geoffrey Chapman, 1981.

Mitchell, L. L. *The Meaning of Ritual.* Connecticut: Morehouse-Barlow, 1988.

Moyo, A. *Zimbabwe: the Risk of Incarnation.* Geneva: W. W. W. Publications, 1996.

Mpofu, E. "Counsellor Role Perceptions and Preferences of Zimbabwe Teachers of a Shona Cultural Background." *Counselling Psychology Quarterly* 7 (1994): 311-326

______. "Exploring the Self-Concept in an African Culture." *Journal of Genetic Psychology* 155 (Sept, 1994): 341-354

Mucherera, Tapiwa. N. *Contextualization of Pastoral Care and Counseling: Reclaiming Shona Indigenous Healing Methods*. M.A. Thesis, Denver, Iliff School of Theology, 1994.

______. "A Historical Perspective to Pastoral Care and Counseling in the United Methodist Church in Zimbabwe Context 1890 to Present." Old Mutare Mission Center, Aug,1997.(unpublished paper),

Mulemfo, M. M. "Palaver as a Dimension of Communal Solidarity in Zaire: A Missiological Study on Transgression and Reconciliation." *Missionalia* 24 (Aug, 1996):129-147.

Mullahy, P. & Melinek, M. *Interpersonal Psychiatry*. New York: SP Medical & Scientific Books, 1983.

Muller, J. "African Contextual Pastoral Theology." *Scriptura* 39 (1991): 77 -88.

Mungadze, J. J. "A Descriptive Study of a Native African Mental Health Problem Known in Zimbabwe as *Zvirwere Zvechivanhu*." *Dissertation Abstracts International* 51 (Mar, 1991): 4272.

Mungazi, Dickson A. *The Mind of Black Africa*. London: Praeger, 1996.

______. *Colonial Policy and Conflict in Zimbabwe: A Study of Cultures in Collision, 1890-1979*. New York: Crane Russak, Taylor and Francis Group, 1992.

Murphree, M. W. *Christianity and the Shona*. London: Atholone Press, 1969.

Musopole, A. C. *Being Human in Africa*. New York, NY: Peter Lang Publishing Inc., 1994.

Mutswairo, S. ed., *Introduction to the Shona Culture*. Kadoma: Juta Zimbabwe Pvt. Ltd., 1996.

Muzorewa, G. H. "A Definition of a Future African Theology." *African Theological Journal* 19 (1990): 168-179.

______. *The Origins and Development of African Theology.* Maryknoll, N.Y.: Orbis Books, 1985.

Mwikamba, C. M. "A search for an African Identity."*AFER-African Ecclesial Review*. (Vol 31, February, 1989): 92.

Myers-James, L., and D. E. Montgomery. "The Development and Validation of an Instrument to Assess an Optimal Afrocentric Worldview." *Journal of Black Psychology* 17 (1990): 37-54.

Namboze, J. L. "Health and Culture in an African Society." *Social Science and Medicine* 17 (1983): 2041-2043.

Nandi, Ashis. *The Intimate Enemy: Loss and Recovery of Self Under Colonialism.* Oxford: Oxford University press, 1983.

Ngara, E. "Language Influence and Culture: Comments on the Impact of English on Shona." *Diogenes* 161 (1993): 27-34.

Niebuhr, H. R. *Christ and Culture*. New York: Harper & Row Publisher, 1956.

Nkurunziza, D. R. K. *Bantu Philosophy of Life in the Light of the Christian Theology*. Frankfurt am Main, Bern, New York, Paris: Peter Lang Publishing Inc., 1989.

Oduyoye, M. A. *Hearing and Knowing: Theological Reflections on Christianity in Africa*. Maryknoll, N.Y.: Orbis Books, 1986.

Ogbonnaya, A. O. *On Communitarian Divinity: An African Interpretation of the Trinity*. New York, NY: Paragon House, 1994.

Okorqcha, C. C. *The Meaning of Religious Conversion in Africa: The Case of the Igbo of Nigeria*. Aldershot: Avebury, 1987.

Okpewho, I. *Myth in Africa: A Study of its Aesthetic and Cultural Relevance*. Cambridge: Cambridge University Press, 1982.

Olupona, J. K. *African Traditional Religion in Contemporary Society*. New York: Paragon House Publication, 1991.

Partain, J. "Christians and Their Ancestors: A Dilemma of African Theology." *Christian Century* 103 (1986): 1066-1069.

Patel, V. "Spiritual Distress: An Indigenous Model of Nonpsychotic Mental Illness in Primary Care in Harare, Zimbabwe." *Acta Psychiatrica Scandinavica* 92 (Aug. 1995):103-107.

Patterson P. R. ed. *The Book of Discipline of the United Methodist Church: Africa Central Conference Edition.* Nashville: The United Methodist Publishing House, 1990.

Pattison, S. *A Critique of Pastoral Care*. London, England: SCM Press Ltd., 1988.

Patton, J. *Pastoral Care in Context: An Introduction to Pastoral Care*. Louisville, KY: Westminister/ John Knox Press, 1993.

Peaden, W. R. *Missionary Attitudes to Shona Culture 1890-1923*. Salisbury (Harare): The Central Africa Historical Association, 1970.

Pedersen, P. B, et al., eds., *Counseling Across Cultures.* (3rd ed). Honolulu: University of Hawaii Press, 1989.

Perrin-Jassy, Marie-France. *Basic Community in the African Churches*. Translated by Sister Jeanne Marie Lyons. Maryknolls, NY: Orbis Books,1973.

Phiri, Millie. "Much has to be Done to Save our Culture." *The Sunday Mail* (August, 25, 1996). C1.

Pobee, J. S. *Towards an African Theology*. Nashville: Abingdon, 1979.

Presler, T. "Missionary Anglicanism Meets an African Religion: A Retrospect of the Centenary of Bishop Knight-Bruce's Entry into Zimbabwe." *Journal of The Southern African Missiological Society* 17.3 (Nov. 1989): 162-175.

Preston, H. *Tsika Dzakanaka*. Gweru: Catholic Mission Press, 1963.

Radcliffe-Brown, A. R. "Taboo," in William A. Lessa and Evon Z. Vogt, eds. *Reader in Comparative Religion: An Anthropological Approach* New York: Harper and Row, 1972.

Radin, P. ed. *African Folktales*. New York: Schocken Books, 1983.

Ranger, T. O., and I. N. Kimamba, eds. *The Historical Study of African Religion*. Los Angeles: University of California Press, 1974.

Rasmussen, L L. *Earth Community Earth Ethics*. Maryknoll, NY: Orbis Books, 1996.

Reagan, C. E. "The Self as Another." *Philosophy Today* 37 (Spring, 1993) 3- 20.

Reynolds, P. *Traditional Healers and Childhood in Zimbabwe*. Athens, Ohio: Ohio University Press, 1996.

Roland, A. *In Search of Self in India and Japan: Towards a Cross-Cultural Psychology*. Princeton: Princeton University Press, 1989.

Romme, M.A. J. "Social Psychiatry in Zimbabwe or the Interplay of Culture and Psychosocial Disorders." *International Journal of Social Psychiatry* 33 (Win, 1987): 263-269.

______. "Culture and Psychosocial Disorder in Zimbabwe," In *Clinical Psychology in Africa (South of the Sahara), the Caribbean and Afro-Latin America: A Textbook for Universities and Paramedical Schools*, eds. K. Peltzer and P. O. Ebigbo. Enugu, Nigeria: S. Asekome & Co., 1989

Ruch, E. A. "African Christianity and African Theology." *Ministry* 11 (1971):116-120.

Ruether, R. R. *Gaia & God: An Ecofeminist Theology of Earth Healing*. New York, NY: Harper Collins Publishers, 1992.

Russell, C. A. *The Earth, Humanity and God: The Templeton Lectures Cambridge.* London, England: UCL Press Ltd., 1994.

Safransky, Sy. "Psychotherapy," *The Yoga Journal* (May/June, 1992): 52 & 53.

Samkange, S. & Samkange, T. M. *Hunhuism or Ubuntuism: A Zimbabwean Indigenous Political Philosophy*. Salisbury (Harare), Zimbabwe: Graham Publishing, 1980.

Sarpong, P. K. B. "Everyday Spirituality in Africa." Ecumenical Review, 38 (Jan, 1986): 4-11.

Schuerkens, U. "The African: an Image Created by the Occident Colonization." *Interculture* (English Edition) 25 (Sum, 1992): 15-25.

Schultz, D. P. & Schultz, S. E. *A History of Modern Psychology*. 4th Ed. San Diego: Hatcourt Brace Jovanovich, Publishers, 1987.

Setiloane, G. M. *African Theology: An Introduction*. Johannesburg, South Africa: Skotaville Publishers, 1986.

Setiloane, G. M. "Where are we in African Theology?" *African Theological Journal* 8 (1979): 7-14.

Shorter, A. *African Culture and the Christian Church.* London: Geoffrey Chapman, 1973.

Shorter, A. "Urbanization: Today's Missionary Reality in Africa." *AFER* 32.5 (Oct. 1990): 290-300.

Shohat, Ella. "Notes on the "Post-Colonial." in *Social Text* Vol. 31/32, (1992), 101.

Shropshire, W. T. *The Church and the Primitive Peoples.* London: Macmillian, 1938.

Sindima, H. "Community of Life: Western Corruption of African Worldview." *Ecumenical Review* 41 (Oct. 1989): 537-551.

Smith, Archie. *Navigating the Deep River: Spirituality in African-American Families.* Ohio: United Church Press, 1997.

Some, M. P. *The Healing Wisdom of Africa: Finding Life Purpose Through Nature, Ritual and Community* New York: Penguin Putnam Inc., 1998.

Spiegel, Y. *The Grief Process: Analysis and Counseling.* Nashville: Abingdon Press, 1977.

Spielberger, C. D., Diaz-Guerrero, R. (eds.) *Cross-Cultural Anxiety Vol 3* Washington, DC: Harper & Row Publisher, 1986.

Ssempija, S. "Needed African Pastoral Psychotherapy." *AFER* 32.3 (June 1990): 150-156.

Stone, H. W. "Sojourn in South Africa: Pastoral Care as a Community Endeavor." *Journal of Pastoral Care* 50 (Sum, 1996): 207-213.

Stone, H. W. *Theological Context for Pastoral Caregiving: Word in Deed.* New York, NY: The Haworth Pastoral Press, 1996.

Stricker, G. ed. *Toward Ethnic Diversification in Psychology Education and Training*. Washington D.C.: American Psychological Association, 1990.

Sue, D. W. & Sue, D. *Counseling the Cultural Different: Theory & Practice*. (2nd Ed.) New York, NY: John Wiley & Sons. Inc., 1990.

Sullivan, H. S. *Personal Psychopathology*. New York: W. W. Norton & Co., 1947.

______. *Concepts of Modern Psychiatry*. New York: W. W. Norton & Co., 1953.

______. *Clinical Studies in Psychiatry*. New York: W.W. Norton & Co., 1956.

______. *Interpersonal Theory of Psychiatry*. New York: W. W. Norton & Co., 1953.

Tessier, R., ed. "Young People in African Towns: Their Pastoral Care." *Missionalia* 13 (Apr: 1985): 45.

Turnbull, C. M. *The Lonely African*. Garden City, N.Y.: Doubleday & Co. Inc., 1962.

van Beek, A. M. *Cross-Cultural Counseling*. Minneapolis, MN: Fortress Press, 1996.

wa Thiongo, N., *Decolonizing the Mind: The Politics of Language in African* Harare: Zimbabwe Publishing House (reprint), 1994.

Wan-Tatah, V. "In Search of a Relevant African Theology Today." In *Footprints: Theological Essays on Church in Cameroon*. ed. Nyansakao ni Nku, Yauonda, (1992):19-45.

Waruta, D. W. ed. *Caring and Sharing: Pastoral Counselling in the African Perspective*. Nairobi Kenya: Act Print Limited, 1995.

Watkins, D., and E. Mpofu. "Some Zimbabwean Evidence of the Internal Structure of the Self Description Questionnaire - 1." *Educational and Psychological Measurement* 54 (Win 1994): 967-972.

Wehrly, B. *Pathways to Multicultural Counseling Competence: A Developmental Journey*. Pacific Grove, CA: Brooks/Cole Publishing Co., 1995.

Weiss, R. S. *Loneliness: The Experience of Emotional and Social Isolation*. Massachusetts, England: The MIT Press, 1973.

Wessels, W. H. "The Traditional Healer and Psychiatry." *Australian and New-Zealand Journal of Psychiatry* 19 (1985): 283-286.

Whidborne, V. A. "Africanisation of Christianity in Zimbabwe." *Religion in Southern Africa* 4 (Jan, 1983): 31-50.

Wicks, R., and Estadt, B.E. eds. *Pastoral Counseling in the Global Church: Voices From the Field*. N.Y.: Maryknoll, Orbis Book, 1993.

Wideman, J. E. *Reclaiming the African Personality*. London, England: Susquehanna University Press, 1995.

Wilson, D. J., and S. Lavelle. "Loneliness and General Psychological Distress Among Zimbabwean Students." *Journal of Social Psychology*: 130 (Apr. 1990): 273-275.

Williams P., & Chrisman, L. *Colonial Discourse and Post-colonial Theory: A Reader*. New York: Columbia University Press, 1994.

Willowghby, W C. *The Soul of The Bantu*. Garden City, NY: Doubleday, Doran & Co. Inc., 1928.

Wimberly, E. P. *Using Scripture in Pastoral Counseling*. Nashville: Abingdon Press, 1994.

______. *Recalling Our Own Stories*. San Francisco, CA: Jossey-Bass Publishers, 1997.

______. *Counseling African American Marriage and Families*. Louisville, K.Y.: Westminster John Knox Press, 1997.

______. *African American Pastoral Care*. Nashville, TN: Abingdon Press, 1992.

______. *Pastoral Counseling and Spiritual Values: A Black Point of View*. Nashville. TN.: Abingdon Press, 1982.

Wiredu, K., and K. Gyekye, eds. *Person and Community*. Washington, D.C.: Cultural Heritage and Contemporary Change Series, Africa, Vol II, 1992.

Wulff, D. M. *Psychology of Religion: Classic and Contemporary Views*. New York, NY: John Wiley & Sons, 1991.

Young, R J. C. *Colonial Desire*. London and New York: Routledge, 1995.

Zvobgo, C. J. M. *A History of Christian Missions in Zimbabwe, 1890-1939*. Gweru, Zimbabwe: Mambo Press, 1996.

______. "Shona and Ndebele Responses to Christianity in Southern Rhodesia, 1897-1914." *Journal of Religion in Africa/Religion en Afrique* 8 (1976): 41-51.

Research in Religion and Family
BLACK PERSPECTIVES

This series aims to provide a framework and opportunity for original research that explores both the ground and the goals of family and religion in the black tradition. Monographs in the series will examine the ways in which kinship networks were formed and maintained, how the community raised and socialized children, how they carved out a religion and fashioned a rich and expressive culture that reflected their uninhibited imagination and provided a means to articulate their hopes and hurts, their dreams and doubts.

Research will not only focus on the past and present, but will also look at the adequacy of current models of family and religion to take the black community into the twenty-first century.

The series editor is:

Noel Leo Erskine
Candler School of Theology
Emory University
Atlanta, GA 30322

To order other books in this series, please contact our Customer Service Department:

(800) 770-LANG (within the U.S.)
(212) 647-7706 (outside the U.S.)
(212) 647-7707 FAX

Or browse online by series:

www.peterlangusa.com